EARLY PRAISE FOR T
CHRONICL

"In the pages of *The Mango Chronicle* you will awaken in a time and place that no longer exists. Cuba before the Castro Revolution was a boy's paradise, as well as his hell in his universal coming-of-age dealing with bullies, then loss, followed with a flight to America to live in an apartment with sixteen others and going to school barely able to speak the language. Many live these experiences; few of us know the intricacies of such a trial by fire. But it is in these boyhood memories of Cuba that Ricardo Gonzalez Rothi defined who he was through a Chevy the color of a plum, an uncle who wears his oddness with grace, the riveting memory of hanging out with the Old Man of the Sea as iconic as the one Hemingway immortalized. As Dr. Ricardo Gonzalez Rothi explores his heritage, we are let into his discovery of compassion and the need to nurture. His carefully carved sentences linger in a reader's mind long after the pages are turned, telling us how he became a man with two souls."

~Shelley Fraser Mickle, Former NPR commentator, author of movie *Replacing Dad*, nominee to the Florida Women's Hall of Fame, author of *Borrowing Life* (Imagine 2020) and the forthcoming *White House Wild Child* (Imagine 2023)

"Mango Chronicles, is a series of masterfully written stories that allow us to join Ricardo through his life journey in Cuba, Mexico, and the United States. I could palpate the emotions, his fears, his loves, and his regrets. This book is a must read, as it not just a great series of stories, but it is about a deeply talented man and what he has accomplished in medicine, as a father and most importantly as an American, it is his life story. I am proud and honored to say he is my friend and colleague. Ricardo, you have elevated us all."

~Pedro José Greer Jr. M.D., Presidential Medal of Honor recipient, author of the memoir, *Waking up in America*

"A complete joy to read, The Mango Chronicle by Ricardo José González Rothi vividly evokes the lost world of pre-Castro Cuba and exquisitely registers the aftershocks of migration. Richly detailed, sharply observed, quietly humorous, and deeply moving, this gentle and sensuous memoir chronicles both the loss of a home and the growth of a soul."

~Joy Castro, PhD**,** Willa Cather Professor of English and Ethnic Studies Director of Institute for Ethnic Studies, University of Nebraska, author of *Flight Risk* (2021) and *One Brilliant Flame* (2023, Lake Union)

"An intimate, heartbreaking, and beautiful narrative about displacement and belonging that captivates you from the very first page. Betty Viamontes, author of the award-winning novel Waiting on Zapote Street."

~Betty Viamontes is the author of four novels and an anthology of short stories. Her novel, *Waiting on Zapote Street* (2015), is a winner of the Latino Books Into Movies Award.

"In The Mango Chronicle we enter the life and world of Ricardo Gonzalez Rothi, whose captivating life story as an impoverished child in Cuba and then a refugee in America is full of wisdom, goodwill, and grace. I will read this memoir-in-essays again both for inspiration and sheer enjoyment. Joelle Fraser, author of The Territory of Men and The Forest House."

~Joelle Fraser is a MacDowell Fellow and the author of two memoirs: *The Territory of Men* (Random House 2002), and *The Forest House: a Journey into the Landscape of Love, Loss and Starting Over* (Counterpoint 2013).

THE MANGO CHRONICLE

RICARDO JOSÉ GONZÁLEZ-ROTHI

The Mango Chronicle

Edited by Lisa Diane Kastner

Published in North America, Australia, and Europe by RIZE. Visit Running Wild Press at www.runningwildpress.com/rize, Educators, librarians, book clubs
(as well as the eternally curious), go to www.runningwildpress.com/rize.

ISBN (pbk) 978-1-960018-19-9
ISBN (ebook) 978-1-960018-15-1

PREFACE

One never stops being a refugee. I still mend my socks when they get a hole. I do not leave any food on my plate. When something I own breaks, I either fix it, or re-purpose it. Nothing is disposed of that could be usable. I still fret with anxiety when going through customs in or out of the country. So this is what I do: When I take a deep breath, I deliberately let the air rush in through my nostrils, let it seep deeply down into my lungs, and then let it out, slowly. I relish the inspiration and feel the power of being untethered and in full control of the exhalation. Breathing is as close a feeling to freedom as I can envision. Freedom, like breathing, is not to be taken lightly. Ask any refugee.

In assimilating to the American way of life, at times I have felt an inexplicable sense of guilt, conflicted that in order to persevere, I have somehow betrayed my birth soul for my "good" American soul. I take comfort, after all these years, in having learned to coexist in two souls. It is a reconciliation of sorts, a delicate balance between displacement and belonging, and between forgetting and forgiveness. Most refugees survive, but not all of us thrive. Any refugee will tell you this also.

Without my family's inspiration and encouragement to push through in spite of the hardships we faced and without the deep spiritual faith and hunger that propelled me to persevere, I might not have thrived. I might not have reached the maturity and inspiration to write this book without the example of my mother, or the mentorship of my teachers who helped me improve my *Inglich*, and inspired me to love reading and to be excited about writing. About ten years ago it occurred to me that there were occurrences in my life, especially of my childhood in Cuba that my wife and two daughters might not have known and would never know unless I jotted down the details. What started as scribbles on napkins, notepads or paper bags I meant to leave for them (you know, just in case...) morphed into a greater need to share with others the message of the life lessons that evolved as I began writing.

After having recently retired from an enriching, albeit intense career in medicine, I am now in my "second chapter" and this has given me time to pause and reflect. It has taken me ten years to shape *The Mango Chronicle*. During that time I have cried over it, savored it, nurtured it, wrote it, re-wrote it, stayed up late with it, but I never gave up on it, just like I never gave up on my patients. Years ago, I rescued a sign from a junk shop. Painted on it are the words, "*I can and I will.*" I placed it on a shelf over my desk at a height where I can just see it every time my eyes wander over my computer screen. It serves as a reminder of always seeking the hope and will to persevere.

I never had the advantage of graduate work in Fine Arts, but my family tells me I have never needed much persuasion to tell a good story. After taking several courses on how to learn the challenging craft of writing I have realized that creativity and "having a story to tell" are not enough to write well; there is much to structure and method. Mrs. Farley, my third-year high school English teacher was right. Nothing comes easy that isn't worth struggling for. I hope you will enjoy reading *The Mango Chronicle* as much as I have delighted in writing it. If you do, please share it. If you don't, I urge you to at least repurpose the paper on which it is written.

Two thirds of author royalties from the proceeds of this book will be contributed to non-profit organizations that promote social justice and freedom around the world. I think of it as one small way to pay it forward.

We all need roots and wings.

To
Mami Lydia, Papi José,
Brother René,
Abuelos Marta and Eradio,
for my roots.

To
Leslie, Elisa and Sara,
because it was you
who gave me wings.

TABLE OF CONTENTS

1
BIENVENIDO

It had been five hard months since we arrived in New Jersey. I used to sit at a turquoise vinyl armchair in the bedroom, where I laid a cut-out piece of plywood over the armrests. That was my desk. We were cramped in a creaky two-story, one-bathroom house where sixteen of us, including my two uncles and their families lived together. With the clunky steam radiator beneath the window, there was hardly space in the room for my parents' double bed and for the trundle bed my six-year-old brother and I shared. That night the pipes in the heater clanged and the air in the room was hot and dry. I woke up, hoping no one would be using the bathroom at five in the morning, got dressed for school and sat quietly in the stair-well, practicing my rudimentary *Inglich* until it was time to eat breakfast. Twenty minutes later I followed my cousin Carlos out the door and onto school. *Vamonos!* It was now late October, cloudy, cold, windy, and miserable. A garbage truck roared past us, trailing what would soon become the familiar stinks and smells of living in the city.

At the end of the school day, at Horace Mann Elementary

they let the seventh graders out first, then the eighth graders. Fists clenched at his sides, Tommy caught up to me and stomped across the street in my direction. He shouted something in English, and before I could react, he shoved me hard into the wall of the synagogue on 85th and 4th. He then grabbed me by the lapels and slammed me onto the sidewalk. My knee caps clacked as they hit concrete.

He tore the front pocket of the coat my *primo* Carlos had lent me. Tommy stepped back, cocked his head, and glared. He was furious and kept shouting. I had no idea what he was saying, but the pain in my knees, the trembling, and the suddenness of it all was so overwhelming, it must have been enough to blunt my understanding of what was happening.

Tommy was a kid in my grade. I did not know him, but I knew he pushed and shoved other kids in the school yard. He had beyond pale white skin and blond-white hair in tight curls, not quite albino, but close. His pale grey eyes bulged as he stared me down. In his three-quarter length black leather jacket, he reminded me of Nazi soldiers I had seen in movies.

It was a bizarre moment. My bones throbbed and in my agony, I could not stop trembling. Still on my knees, I reached for my splattered books as Tommy loomed over me. Gathering my papers and books was the only submissive thing I could think to do because I thought he was about to kick me in the face. But he didn't. He towered over me for what felt like forever, but may have been only a few seconds.

I planted one foot forward as if genuflecting and then, lowering my right arm as I stood, I hooked the pasty *cabrón* with a tight fist. I missed his chin, but made contact, as I felt his front teeth scrape my ungloved knuckles. The blood on my fist was not only mine. In reaction to my punch, Tommy stumbled back a step, cupped his nose with both hands and lowered his head. Blood gushed from his nose and dripped onto the concrete.

Shit, shit...you goddamn-fucking SPIC. You SPIC!

Still stunned and not sure of what brought all this on, I rescued what books I could and ran down 85th street towards *tio's* house. Tommy didn't follow me. He walked off in the opposite direction, bleeding and cursing, stomping his feet, and clutching his face. As I looked over my shoulder, he launched the middle finger of his gloved right hand in my direction.

He shouted something to the effect of *You don't belong here, you fucking banana-boat, shit-eating SPIC! Go back the fuck where you came from!!*

As I reached the steps of Tio Carlos' house I realized I must have peed my pants during the ordeal. I looked down at my chest. Over where my heart lay, the torn pocket of my cousin's jacket still clung to the coat, dangling like a limp tongue. Blood spattered on my hands, on the coat, and all over my book covers. The ragged cuts on my bare knuckles stung in the cold air. I just sat there on the second step of my uncle's stoop. It felt like I wanted to cry but my ribs hurt and I couldn't catch my breath. I stood, went around the back of the house and washed Tommy's blood off my hands.

I hated the New Jersey streets, the naked trees, the drab red brick, and brown stones of the houses with concrete for yards, the dented garbage cans on the curb, the dogshit on the sidewalk, the graffiti. I hated the cold wind and the ever-grey skies. I hated that all the houses in the neighborhood had steps to climb to the front door. I hated the moldy-smelling basements and the honking cars day and night, and the people who didn't say hello back or smile. I hated not understanding what they said.

I never told my parents what had happened that afternoon. I went to bed that night, fretting whether Tommy would be waiting for me outside school in the morning, and would I have the strength to defend myself if he decided to attack me again. I started praying *Santa Maria, madre de Díos*... The cut on my knuckles stung and my kneecaps ached from where Tommy had slammed me onto the sidewalk. I couldn't help but start to sob under my blanket and I must have dozed off from the exhaustion.

Sometime during early morning, while still dark, I awoke and realized I must have been dreaming about being back home. Lying there on my back, staring at the ceiling, I began to remember all kinds of things, like the time at my friend Juanito's parents' finca on the outskirts of the *Ciudad of Matanzas*, when we climbed a large mango tree that his *abuelo* had planted behind their house. The tree which grew on a bank, overlooked a stream on the edge of tall cow grass. This tree had to be quite old, as even as a tall nine-year-old, I could not wrap my arms around the trunk. The bottom branches were worn from years of friends and relatives of Juanito's family trying to climb it, and the broken branches looked more like stubby knobs. The knobs made it easier for not-so-good tree climbers like me and Juanito to reach the higher branches.

I remember how we sat with our backs against the large branches that split off from the main trunk, feet braced on the knobs below. We picked only the ripest and yellowest fruit, cupping it in one palm, and pounding the fruit against the trunk to soften the flesh inside. After a while, the fruit became soft as the pulp inside became mushy beneath the leathery skin of the mango. When squeezing the fruit from the bottom upwards, nicking the skin of the fruit with our teeth, sweet-scented juice would ooze out. We ate mangos until the sweetness became near-sickening, or until our hands became so sticky that bees landed on our knuckles, trying to get to the spilled yellow nectar. In our carefree world, the supply of mangos was endless.

Those days of sitting in the arms of the old mango tree, of feeling the salty Cuban breeze touch my face, of hearing the shiny green leaves shiver on its branches while we told each other stories and talked about what we would become when we grew up seemed so distant from the moment. But the moment felt so good. I missed my friend.

When I thought of that sunny life back just a few months before, the drab days of now, and all that has passed since we came to New Jersey, I felt half-full, half-empty. What happened to Juanito? Was the old mango tree still there? In my memory, I was taken back to its branches, to the rich soil that embraced its roots. I began to feel sorry for myself now that my own roots felt like they had been ripped apart. *Would I just become another nameless extranjero emigrante dropped onto the sidewalks of New Jersey?* The alarm on mami's night table went off and mami woke my brother up.

After lining up and waiting for turns in the bathroom, I finally crossed the threshold and shut the door behind me. On the cover of a magazine on the floor by the toilet, was a picture of a white-bearded man, with a white star on his top hat, a blue coat, and a red tie, pointing his finger. It was like this *gringo,* dressed in red, white, and blue came to life and was staring at me. He was dressed in the colors of *my* Cuban flag. Maybe he was trying to tell me something. *In time,* I thought, *my Cuban blood will become American blood.*

2
FOTOS

I recently found a handful of photos that my relatives sent to the U.S. after we left Cuba as refugees. One in particular: a black-and-white glossy of a boy who was bare-chested and stood inside a chicken coop in his play shorts and leather high-top shoes. The boy smiled, one foot planted forward with hand outstretched towards a curious rooster. The bird's beak was one inch from the boy's hand. Scribbled on the back of the photograph was "*Ricardito, patio de Abuela, Noviembre 1953*." The little boy was me. I have no reason to think the rooster might have pecked at my hand, since looking at the image all these years has never triggered anxiety—and I have always loved chickens.

I do not remember who might have captured the scene, but the feelings I get when I look at this photograph are so intense that, even a half-century later, the rooster's tail feathers feel eerily palpable. I have always considered the gentle sense of place evoked by this image as defining what I first remember of my childhood. What I am about to tell you is what I remember, as I remember it, acknowledging that some memories might have been tainted by the passing of time, by some perhaps-not-so-accurate-recollections, and by a number of gaps along the way.

3
LA CASITA

I spent most of my childhood at *abuela's* house. Abuela was my mother's mother. The house was simple: whitewashed stucco with a large, two-panel heavy wood door-to-ceiling front door with iron hinges and large lion-head shaped knockers. The living room had Moorish style garnet and gold tile floors and the rooms in the rest of the house had coarse flagstone floors throughout. I craved the coolness of the stone floors where abuela would usually find me sprawled out, deeply asleep on the stones with my toy soldiers spread about me.

All the rooms opened out to a long, narrow courtyard. At the end was the kitchen. This *cocina* had a stone charcoal pit with an iron grill on which all food was cooked, water was boiled and *café con leche* was made. Wooden shelves above served as storage space for dishes. Large burlap bags filled with Cuban staples like rice, red, black, and pinto beans were stored beneath the countertop. Pots and pans hung from the ceiling over the grill.

Ricardito, bring me an onion and some parsley from the garden. When abuela stood at the grill, it was impossible not to tug her skirt and beg for a little piece of *bistec*. The pungent smell of lime juice and fresh pepper, the sound of the garlic-laden skirt steak as it sizzled on her hot iron pan sending puffs of flavor into the kitchen was overwhelming.

Here, she would say, *You scrub this potato and wash it, then we peel it and cut it. We can fry the little pieces with salt and olive oil like you like it.*

I would eventually learn to set mousetraps behind the grain-filled sacks in fruitless attempts to control the mice her cooking attracted and which considered the kitchen their cantina.

Abuela...look! We caught a ratón! But...it's not moving.

Can you take it off the mousetrap? she would say, *But first let's get some more stinky cheese to bait it again.*

But abuela, I would say, *Do mice go to heaven?*

Only if you bury them. So, I would bury them.

The courtyard of what became my childhood playground opened into a square backyard, which was mostly dirt, but which was flanked on either side by beautiful rose, herb, and flower gardens. If plants were the love, passion, and pride of my abuela, raising chickens was abuelo's obsession. In the backyard was a round pen for training his fighting cocks. There was the chicken coop described in the *fotos*, and a pig pen which were the sources of our fresh meat supplies, given the absence of niceties of modern living like freezers and supermarkets in those days.

Time to clean up the pigeon coop, Uncle Yayo would say, handing me a scoop, a brown paper bag and hoisting me up the little wooden ladder. *Make sure you scrape all the corners real good.* In one corner of the yard there was a large pigeon coop built on a platform atop the rabbit hutches. My uncle, a school-teacher and bachelor who lived with my grandparents raised fancy rabbits and trained carrier pigeons as one of his many eccentric hobbies.

We had no air conditioning and no telephone, but we had running water, electricity, and an indoor toilet. The house had a Spanish tile roof over the main part, and a corrugated tin roof over the kitchen. My grandparents owned three oscillating GE table fans, the only refrigerator on the block, a Frigidaire, and a seafoam green Phillips shortwave radio which adorned the living room.

Mamá, make sure Ricardito never tells anyone we have this radio, my grandfather would remind abuela on an almost weekly basis. That Phillips radio would eventually become our family's conduit to the free world during *Voz of America* broadcasts after Fidel's revolution. These items constituted the sum of household luxuries in my grandparents' house.

The courtyard on the side of the house had a concrete slab. It was the hub of my uncle's eclectic menagerie, with over twenty homemade bird cages hanging from the eaves, filled with colorful and melodious finches, grassquits, mockingbirds, bluebirds, cardinals, and other tropical birds that he trapped, bred and collected. Every time any of my friends came to visit at abuela's house, Uncle Yayo would warn us,

Keep your fingers and your friends' fingers away from the cage! He bites!

Ok, tío, but how come he never bites you?

My uncle had built a large cage which housed his prized pet, an untamed squirrel monkey. He also had several fish tanks teaming with tropical fish. Then there were the clay pots and planters exploding with bougainvilleas and night-blooming *jasmín* whose branches crept over the stone wall flanking the courtyard, separating it from the house next door. The animals were my uncle's realm, but the flora of the yard, and the splendor of the many flowers in it were my grandmother's and the honeybees.'

One day abuelo came in the house.

Mamá, I'm here...I can't stay too long. The orange bus has a flat tire.

He had come home for lunch as he did every day, and after abuela served him a hot meal and he finished eating, all of a sudden, he pulled his teeth out of his mouth, dunked them in a glass of water, rinsed them-then put them back in his mouth. I was shocked at how someone could pull so many teeth out at the same time and put them back in without crying or bleeding... like when *papi* pulled mine. I did not know about dentures and abuelo never let on, making me feel like he was a wizard, and this was a special magic trick of his. The thought of his toothless grin always brings me back to that special table. Abuela's table was in a multipurpose room adjacent to the kitchen, as the kitchen was too small to sit in and the ceiling was low. Her table was of heavy, unvarnished *majagua* wood, the same wood that professional baseball bats were made of. When the table wasn't used for meals, my uncle used it as a worktop or a desk.

Ricardito, please hand me the camisas from the clothesline if they are dry, abuela said.

I pulled them off, saved the clothespins and brought in the clean shirts. The old table was the place where my grandmother folded laundry. It was the place where my mother sat and mended my socks, or around which my father and uncles sat on Saturday nights drinking *cafecitos* (super sugar-saturated expresso black Cuban coffee) till the late hours as they mostly laughed, argued baseball and boxing, and it was where I learned to play dominoes.

On the same table, every day my grandmother placed a large tin tub full of lukewarm water, and bathed me prior to putting me down for my ritual midday nap. She combed my hair with violet water, rubbed cornstarch on my chest and trunk, so I wouldn't stick to the sheets during my daily siesta in the room next door. Abuela's house was where I first began to grow my roots.

4
AN ENIGMA IN PARENTHESES

No one could come within five feet of it. The "plum" as the neighbors called it, was a 1951 maroon, four door Chevrolet, with gray cloth seats. He kept the car on *calle Cuba*, but it seemed like anytime he took it out, he had to have a person guarding it. That person would be me.

Keeping a lookout for that maroon Chevy made me proud, but also scared me a little because if anything happened to the car while I watched it, it would be my fault. Uncle Yayo bought a special washcloth and he bragged that it was made from leather from an animal from Africa. Two or three times a week, he filled a bucket with water, and put exactly three drops of kerosene in the water. If he put more than that, he would dump the bucket and start over. He used the soft leather thing to wet, wipe and shine the car with it. Uncle Yayo said that the kerosene made it shiny and took off any dirt from the road- and that it did.

One day, Uncle Yayo let me sit next to him up in the front seat. I was around eight years old and could barely see over the dashboard. Riding in the front seat with my uncle made me feel special. But the car stopped suddenly, wheels screeched. I shot forward, but his arm kept me from getting hurt. A stray dog had jumped out in front of us, but he didn't kill the dog. And he didn't yell at me for almost banging my head, although I was scared and started crying. Instead, he leaned me back on the seat, grabbed the stick below the steering wheel, jiggled it and stepped on the pedals on the floor. The Chevy went forward nice and smooth-like, like nothing had happened. It was nothing like when abuelo drove the clunky old bus, as the thing always clanked, jerked and groaned as it picked up speed.

Like I said, just sitting in the front seat of my uncle's Chevrolet, I felt important, but that was nothing compared to the day a couple of years later that he sat me on his lap and let me have my first turn at steering-while the car was moving. I never told this to my parents, because I knew they would have never let me go out with him again, and never let me be his car security guard not ever. Since he was little my uncle had epileptic fits and back then in Cuba, I don't think anyone cared whether you got into a car and drove.

My uncle's real name was Eradio. "Yayo" was his nickname, that's what my Uncle Carlos called him. Carlos was his little brother, and mami said when Carlos was a baby, he could not say his name, "Eradio." The best he could do was "Yayo." The name stuck. Uncle Yayo was one of the smartest people I have ever met. He was also very strange. The oldest of my abuela and abuelo's kids, my grandmother said he was always sickly as a child. He was real skinny and had a large head with jet-black wavy hair, and big ears which stuck out, elephant-like from either side of his head. He had no hair on his face and so he never had to shave. He was so strange that instead of brilliantine, like most men and boys used on their hair back then, instead he rubbed olive oil through his hair every couple of days *to keep it shiny and silky*. I think my Uncle Yayo was not the most macho-looking Cuban boy growing up, and maybe that's why he wasn't good at being around people, especially the girls. Mami said he never had a girlfriend.

It probably didn't help Yayo that my grandfather was pretty strict. He wanted his boys to be tough and to never back away from anything. Skinny as my uncle was, I suppose that like me, Uncle Yayo was always the one picked on as he was growing up, so instead of using his muscles, I believe Uncle Yayo got through being a kid by staying to himself and using his brain instead. He would be what nowadays kids would call a geek or nerd. But in my mind, he was neither of those things.

To me, my Uncle Yayo was someone I respected, but he was not someone I liked or would have had as a friend. He was hard to be around, because of all his strange habits and strong personality. But he knew everything about everything. And I mean everything. He learned to drive one of abuelo's buses at age 14, had to sit on a crate and could barely reach the pedals. If my grandfather had found out that Moreno the mechanic taught my uncle to drive, he would have fired Moreno. Uncle Yayo could fix a carburetor, patch tires, upholster the seats by the time he was 16; all from watching others do things just once or twice.

Tío, why did you become a teacher?

I don't know why. Your abuelo said we didn't have the money for me to go to Habana to study at the universidad, but he said I could go to the Escuela Normal in Matanzas and live at home if I wanted. So, I did. That's all. That is why I became a teacher.

The *Escuela Normal* was a teacher's college. It was also where my mother would study to be a teacher. After he finished, Yayo taught classes in the small town of Aguacate, and later he and my mother started a little school there. This was a very poor country town where parents did not believe in their kids wasting time to sit in front of books, but rather they were in the fields, working with their hands.

It took some time, but Uncle Yayo began convincing parents around Aguacate that what he taught their kids wasn't just about book stuff. He taught them that in order for them to build a fence or a chicken coop, or to space corn or to figure out how many seeds they needed to plant a field of a certain size, then they needed to learn to measure, count, add and subtract the lengths of things. They needed to know about inches and square feet... They needed to know how to sign their names and learn to read.

One of his favorite school lessons started by telling his students that if they found a dead animal then they should wrap it in something and bring it to school. He said no dead dogs because they could have rabies. Uncle Yayo would cut open the animals, and show the students where the organs were, explained what each organ did, and where muscles, bones, and joints were. He told them if they learned about this, they then they could know how to help butcher *jutias*, a rabbit or a chicken, or how to fix the broken leg of an animal. He explained how living things were put together in a very simple and fun way. After cutting open an animal, he showed the kids how to preserve them, by stuffing the dead animal while they were in class instead of burying it. Most kids loved this.

Yayo mounted all of the animals he stuffed around the classroom. He asked the students to make drawings of them and write stories about them. He had taught himself how to draw and did beautiful pencil drawings. He hand-printed the names on all the graduation diplomas for the school with pen and ink like in the real fancy, private school diplomas. The kids and their moms and dads loved to see their names in fancy loopy letters on a diploma. I guess it made them feel not poor.

My uncle was very picky and stiff about everything he did

and with everything he owned. He wore the same light grey suit (I think it was the only one he owned) to school every day. He ironed it and mended the sleeves and buttons himself. And he always wore starched shirts my grandmother washed and ironed for him for the week. Yayo owned two ties and switched them every other day, always with the same routine. Even what he ate every day was the same.

My friends asked me how I could be around an odd-looking and strange man like my uncle, who had such weird habits, especially when he wasn't always nice to me and always rode me hard to do things just the way he wanted. Besides, he was very stubborn and picky. I never totally understood what mami meant when she said, *He is your mentor and your tormentor* because I was a kid and I assumed I had to do as he said because he was an adult. But mami, like me, always tolerated him. It was like she always took care of him. Anyway, I don't know why or how I stuck by him. It wasn't that I felt sorry for him or anything like that. I guess all I could say was that he let me spend time and do things with him, time that my father didn't have because he was always so busy working in the *bodega*.

My Uncle Yayo taught me to pull and straighten nails, hammer nails, use a saw, measure and cut wood. I spent many hours beside him as his helper and I always did whatever he asked me to do. By the time I was around twelve years old, I became really good at cutting and nailing wire mesh for chicken coops and even making hinges from sheet metal. He also taught me to cut glass with a glass cutter. He was great at building fish tanks, for which he cut glass from old windows people threw away and set them in concrete.

Here, Ricar, put this on the bottom of the tank and spread it. Tío gave me handfuls of crushed charcoal to spread on the bottom of the fish tanks. He had me place small river pebbles over the charcoal. He said this would keep the water fresh and clean. We also collected plants and large snails from the springs near the Yumurí river to place in the fish tanks.

Tío, why do you put th plants and the snails in the tank?

That is so the fish think they are still in the river. It also helps the baby fish hide from the bigger fish so they don't get eaten and the snails clean the glass. Uncle Yayo had all the fish tanks hooked up to one another with small hoses which always had a trickle of running water, with the last one dumping water and fish poop out into the garden. He said it made good fertilizer for abuela's flowers. In these fish tanks he had hundreds of tropical fish and the water in them looked as clear as that of the natural springs. We used old mosquito nets and he took me to the springs on the edge of the city where we scooped up mollies and beautiful guppies in the currents. Uncle Yayo sometimes gave away fish to the kids in the neighborhood who wanted to have a fish tank, and those he didn't give away, we put back in the stream.

I learned all about breeding fish from Uncle Yayo. He also taught me how to stuff a dead fish. My first one was a red snapper that my grandmother bought from the fishmonger. I remember how scared I was pulling out the fish's guts after making a cut along the bottom, and how disgusted I was at the smell of fish on my hands and as the scales stuck to my fingers. I teased out the skin, cut out all the fish meat carefully, and cleaned out the guts and everything down to the bones. With old scissors, Uncle Yayo taught me how to clip the vertebra off and remove the skeleton except for the skull; then with a syringe, I had to squirt a liquid called formaldehyde into the skull and scoop out both eyes; then rinse out the cleaned-out skin attached to the fish's head and tail, and stuff it with formaldehyde-soaked cotton balls. He did the stitching of the skin and helped me mold the fish back to its shape with a wire from head to tail so the body could be curved into a position to look like it was swimming.

We hung the fish under the eaves of the house where it got a fresh breeze but neither got rained on or straight sun. Tio said that this was to make the formaldehyde pickle the body for several weeks. During that time the fish lost its fishy smell but stank instead of formaldehyde for weeks. After a while, I got really upset about my fish because the red snapper colors turned grey and yellowish and went dry, like the salted *bacalao* papi sold in his store. But Uncle Yayo told me to have patience, that he could fix the colors. After a few more days, my uncle used enamel paint and began putting back the colors of the skin and scales to look like a live fish, with bright pinks and reds. He painted the fins with thin black lines; the eyes he made out of glass buttons from abuela's sewing basket and he glued the glass buttons into the eye sockets and then painted the black pupil on the eye. The eyes looked so real. He put varnish over the dried enamel. It was like my snapper came alive. I was a very proud twelve-year-old after doing my first fish-stuffing project.

It was a sad day when we left Cuba one year later and my uncle had to turn his Chevrolet to the government authorities. Back then, when you left Cuba as an exile, you had to turn in all your belongings, bank account, house, car, etc. to Fidel Castro's revolutionary government. Uncle Yayo never said a word the day he returned from the *Jefatura de la Revolución* after giving the keys and papers of his Chevrolet to the bearded *miliciano* behind the desk. He walked about fifteen blocks back to abuela's house, wearing his grey suit and maroon tie in the heat of the day. When he got home, he looked like he had been in the rain, but it was all sweat. He must have known he would never see his "plum" again and that no one else could take care of that car the way he did. It was like someone in his family died. He didn't speak to anybody for days, just moped around.

My uncle's car was really the one thing he owned that made him who my uncle wanted to be. I think it was the way he wanted people in the neighborhood to see him. Driving his shiny plum while he wore his suit was his way of putting aside all the bad feelings he felt, of feeling like he didn't fit in a town that didn't much tolerate people who were funny-looking and weird like he was and who, without notice peed themselves, bit their tongues, and passed out after having jerking fits.

5
LAGRIMITAS

Mami used to tell people that I was a very delicate boy. My parents instilled in me to do right and to avoid hurting others. I took it to heart. I always assumed that if I treated people the way I wanted to be treated, people around me would do likewise. It was the golden rule.

The golden rule. Little did I know that this moral imperative would be seriously challenged within a few short years of exposure to other kids in my barrio, especially in unsupervised settings, like on the alleys and empty lots off Medio, Guachinango, and San Gabriel Streets. I was the youngest of a group of boys that wandered about the *calles* in my neighborhood. This was our playground.

Rique, Oscar, Félix, Vento, Pupi, Armando, Generoso, and Helio were at least three or four years older than me. They attended the same public school in our neighborhood. I took the bus to Irene Toland School, a private school run by the *Presbiterianos* in the Simpson neighborhood, on the outskirts of Matanzas. At Irene Toland, most of the kids were paired in classes with the same age kids and supervised by gentle, but discipline-inclined teachers. I had some run-ins with other kids from time to time at school, but short of name-calling and a shove here and there, I rarely encountered kids who didn't share consensus in the golden rule.

In my barrio of Matanzas Oeste, things were different. I soon learned that finding my place among a group of kids in the neighborhood came with a complex set of herd behaviors. To say that I was beyond naïve was a gross understatement. I was drawn into fights I didn't provoke, pushed into puddles I didn't intend to step in, blamed for stealing or breaking things I neither stole nor broke. Because I was younger, I became the by-default recipient of most nefarious happenings. Whenever there was a need to blame someone for something gone wrong, I became the *de facto* perpetrator.

It didn't help that my father was a well-respected businessman in the neighborhood who had no tolerance for me being out of line, even in unprovoked situations where I might have been trying to defend myself. My father embraced a "customer is always right" and "turn the other cheek" philosophy which I suspect served him well with his customers. He was a polite, albeit big and muscular man who exuded and demanded respect, and who actively avoided altercations. What this meant for me was that if I ever took a swing at any of the neighborhood kids, even in self-defense, and a parent ever came to complain about me to my father, it didn't matter who did what, or when. I was always in the wrong.

It was under such tenuous circumstances that my childhood socialization coping mechanisms soon imploded. The boys in the neighborhood nick-named me "Lagrimitas" ("*little tears*" in Spanish). And so it was that whenever my face became the target of a flying fist or my knee the substrate for an asphalt confrontation from an ill-intentioned shove, I had to suck it up: *Don't fight back, turn the other cheek, succumb to the misery of passivity, and walk off quietly, hold back the sobs, try to hide the anger, pain, and frustration that comes from humiliation and helplessness.* That was it. But holding back tears was contrary to the physiology of the moment.

It also didn't help that I was not a meat eater. According to my mother, I was *anémico and asténico* because of this. I was what some would describe as a wimpy, scrawny kid. I used to faint at the sight of blood, and was known to collapse when overheated. In contrast, the rest of the kids in the barrio were tough, street-hardened kids. Félix was the most macho and Pupi, at age 13 looked and smelled like Kid Gavilán, the legendary Cuban welterweight champion. Pupi had glistening blue-black skin and well-developed muscles on his arms and torso. He even had bulging muscles on his forehead and neck and hair in his underarms.

Despite being skinny, I was a good technical boxer and I could outrun any kid in Matanzas Oeste, except for Armando, who was 15 and already had facial hair. Abuelo taught me to punch well, but the accuracy of my punches was consistently undermined by the lack of impact force behind them. And so it was: if I was to co-exist in the barrio, I had no choice but to have hope for the golden rule. But just in case, as I perfected the art of turning the other cheek, I also learned to run fast whenever I had to.

Then there was Helio. A habitual brawler, Helio would put my golden rule to the test on several occasions. A head of curly black hair topped his greasy forehead, and tufts of unruly eyebrows rimmed a pair of beady, menacing eyes. When he spoke, a stench of rotting meat seeped out between and around a mouth busied by thick lips and several missing teeth. He was short and stocky and rolled his sleeves over his biceps.

Helio was an only child. His father was a bricklayer who drank *aguardiente* on a regular basis. Everyone in the neighborhood knew Helio's father beat him regularly, sometimes for no obvious reason. I overheard mami talk with neighbors about Helio's mother not being a very motherly woman. I think Helio had no one in his family to teach him about the golden rule or the importance of cheek-turning. But I lacked the intellectual maturity to rationalize this at the time, so I couldn't help but dislike him intensely.

I don't know, but Helio was an angry person whose purpose in life it seemed, was about stealing fruit from La Plaza market or skipping school or even beating up people like me who could not defend themselves. Most of the other neighborhood kids tolerated him but no one ever sought him out to play.

They say that every person has his day of reckoning. My Uncle Yayo was greatly instrumental in allowing my day of reckoning to materialize. He knew that I was being bullied by someone in the neighborhood. Uncle Yayo sensed that I had withdrawn for several days. I came home from school and found excuses not to play outside. He asked me if something was wrong, and although I tried to avoid the topic, the lagrimitas on my face would ultimately betray me.

Uncle Yayo told me that as a child he had been bullied. He told me that his Uncle Luis gave him a solution to the problem and that although he knew my father wouldn't approve of it, he felt it was time for him to intervene on my behalf. I was mortified. I didn't want my uncle to embarrass me in front of the neighborhood kids by trying to defend me.

The next day when I stopped to see Tío Yayo he said he had something for me. From the glove compartment of his Chevrolet he pulled out an object which was wrapped in brown paper, and tied neatly with twine. It was about four inches by one and triangle-shaped. When he handed it to me, it felt dense. I suspected it was a rock wrapped in paper. Indeed it was a chunk of heavy, white marble.

Keep this in your back pocket at all times, he said.... *The next time anyone does something really bad to you, you just quietly stand up, take a step back, slide your fingers into your back pocket and smile...*

Smile for what? I said.

You smile to make him think you are not angry. At the same time, you are gripping your rock tightly in your hand and you are positioning yourself just far enough not to be reached by the bully, but not too far to miss your target, said Yayo.

You mean, you expect me to throw the rock at him? Is that what you mean?

No, not exactly. I want him to catch the rock that you will be pitching to him as fast and as hard as you can throw it. If he is not quick enough to catch it, then it becomes his problem. Then you apologize politely and walk away... That is what Uncle Yayo said to do.

I was totally confused. I could not believe my uncle, a highly respected teacher was telling me to do this. Urging me to deliberately hurt someone went counter to everything mami, papi and abuela ever taught me. At the same time, however, I was desperate. I felt trapped in my own anemic, asthenic and scrawny body. I had had it with hiding from Helio when I got home from school. The taunts and shouts of *Here comes Lagrimitas, crying down the street...are you going to hide under your mami's blusa?* were more than I could take. Now that I was almost ten, I didn't like the idea that girls in the neighborhood would see me crying and running away—especially Catia. I put the rock in my back pocket and headed home. That night I hid it under my pillow so mami wouldn't see it. The next morning, I hid it under the mattress and when I came home from school and changed into my playclothes, I placed the rock in my right rear pocket.

As I went outside that day, I felt different somehow. I knew

I wouldn't likely do what my uncle suggested, for it was not my nature to be violent, but I felt more secure knowing that I had protection. I noticed I began to walk differently. I looked up instead of at the ground. I swung my arms with *confianza y seguridad*, instead of letting them dangle by my side.

Several weeks went by. There were no confrontations, no taunts from the kids. I began to think there was something special about my rock, that perhaps it was a talisman and that it protected me from the taunts and the bullying while still let me apply the golden rule and avoid becoming the neighborhood pincushion. I had to get new paper to re-wrap the rock every two or three days, as the sweat from my body and the friction from playing frayed the wrapping.

One day, several of the kids had been talking and bragging about birds they had trapped in the fields. We called these small finch-like birds *tomeguines* (grassquits). Prized for their beautiful song, many people in Matanzas trapped and kept these little birds as pets in homemade cages and aviaries.

Uncle Yayo, who built bird cages out of river reeds, helped me build my trap cage. This trapping cage had a center compartment, in which a male bird would be placed as a decoy. *Tomeguines* are very territorial, and a singing male attracted other birds. On the side compartments of the cage there were rocking trap doors onto whose edges I glued thistle seeds. Birds attracted by the decoy's song would land on the cage and hop towards the rocker panels in search of the seed. Upon landing on the rockers, their own body weight would push the rocker doors and they would fall through to the bottom of the trap, unharmed, but unable to flee.

Others in the neighborhood had similar traps. We went out to the sugar cane fields early on weekends to trap the prized songbirds. By days' end it was common to return to find ten or twenty *tomeguines* in our cages. We traded, sold, or kept the best birds, and let the others go.

I brought out my cage to show the kids a *tomeguín* I had trapped two days earlier at Juanito's father's farm. Uncle Yayo said he was an unusually fine bird, with the loudest and sweetest song he had ever heard. I placed the cage on the edge of the sidewalk at the base of the steps of the butcher's shop. My little *tomeguín* with the olive-green body, fiery yellow breast and shiny black beak hopped to-and-fro in the cage. I knelt against the curb, with the cage in front of me. Rique and Oscar and Félix and Helio sat on the steps, with Helio nearest to the sidewalk.

As I began to tell them where I had trapped this bird, the little *tomeguín* started to chirp excitedly, then went into a singing flurry. The boys were amazed, as was I, at how loud, crisp and clear this little bird's song was. That is, all except Helio. He looked down with disdain at the cage, and as he uncurled his legs out from under him, he puckered up and spit on my cage. He then kicked the cage off the sidewalk with his right leg. I fell back onto the street, trying to catch the tipping cage.

I eased the cage onto the curb, then stood up slowly. Helio glared at me.

Don't you start to cry, now, Lagrimitas...You can just take your little tomeguín and shove it up your... Helio seethed. He shouted so close to me that I could smell his foul spittle as it sprayed my face.

I stepped back, smiled and reached with my hand around to my back pocket, just like Tío Yayo said. In one single, smooth motion I put my left foot forward, leaned back slightly, as I unsheathed the rock. All I can remember was an uncontrollable fury unfurled inside. In a blur I swung my arm forward with a strength I never before experienced. I flung the rock at Helio. His groin got in the way.

In utter disbelief, Helio looked at me and tried to lunge. His fists were curled, his rotten teeth showed, eyes glaring. But as he tried to get to his feet, his eyes rolled upwards in a most unusual way, like a doll's eyes. He grunted, exhaled, fell to his knees, and then fell face down onto the concrete sidewalk. His arms lay curled below his hips. Helio lay there, limp like an abandoned marionette.

They all thought I had killed him. He wasn't moving. A man across the street ran towards us, lifted Helio up and put him in a car with the help of a woman passerby. They took him away. The other three boys stood silent, arms at their sides, looking like they'd just seen a ghost.

I knew what I had done. I thought of my father. I thought I would go to jail. Then I thought I would go to hell for having killed Helio and that God would never forgive me.

I ran up the street to abuela's house and slammed the front door shut, panting heavily. My heart raced. I felt flushed. My chest was tight and my fingers tingled. This time there were no tears. Leaning behind the closed front door, I felt an ugly calm inside. I had left my trap cage and my little bird by the curb. But I felt like the whole neighborhood knew what a terrible thing I had done. I could not go back out in the street.

I stayed at abuela's house until it was dark and then scrambled to the apartment behind papi's grocery. I didn't eat my dinner that night. Luckily, papi had been at a Chamber of Commerce meeting since earlier that afternoon, so he didn't come home until after I was in bed and he didn't know about Helio. Mami also did not know what had happened because abuela had not told her. I buried my face in a comic book after draping my mosquito net over the posts on the bed when mami came to kiss me good night. She must have assumed I was asleep, turned out the light and closed the door. I laid awake in the darkness for most of the night. No tears.

The next morning I left for school. No news of Helio. The police had not come to arrest me yet. I prayed at the Irene Toland Chapel, but I felt no remorse. All I could feel in my heart was an empty, emotionless dark space.

When I got off the bus from Irene Toland School that afternoon, my father stood at the corner, waiting for me. Helio's father was there, as was Helio's mother. Several neighbors were around them, including Oscar and Rique and Félix. None of them could look me straight in the face. I scanned for the familiar drab tan uniform of Matanzas policemen, but there were none in sight.

My father said nothing. He twisted my ear in front of all those people and dragged me inside the grocery store. He slid off his leather belt as he pulled me into my bedroom.

I felt no pain. The sound of the leather snapping in mid-air before it struck was welcomed. I deserved punishment. I realized then, as I laid face down on my bed, accepting my father's anger and feeling the sting of the leather on my buttocks that Helio must not have died. Still no tears. Ugly calm inside.

I found out later that night from my parents that Helio went to the hospital, that the neighborhood kids who were there explained to Helio's mother and father what had happened. My father implored Helio's parents not to call the police. They didn't. Papi promised them I would be punished by being confined to my room for a month and that this would never happen again.

The month went by. My father did not speak to me for the whole time. I came home from school, changed into my playclothes and sat on my bed. I read comic books and drew cartoons to ward off the boredom. I thought many times about escaping out the window and running to abuela's. I thought about running away from home altogether. Twice I packed some clothing, a penknife and some candy and fashioned a bundle with a shirt whose long sleeves I knotted together and looped as a handle. I was ready to escape, but I didn't. I was afraid.

I didn't know what happened to my *tomeguín* or my trap cage after the incident. I was not allowed to visit or talk to abuela or abuelo, or to my Uncle Yayo, or to play with my dog, Yuti. My mother never spoke about the incident, but somehow I wished she knew how I felt.

After the month of home imprisonment ended, I felt both relieved and scared to be free. I didn't know what would happen. Would Helio be waiting to ambush me? Had he been plotting to kill me? What would the neighborhood kids do?

They were all playing hide-and-go-seek on the early evening of my release. I walked down the street eating shaved ice with coconut syrup from a paper cone. I sat on the curb near where Félix was counting. The other boys ran off to find places to hide. Félix looked over his shoulder towards me *Ocho, nueve y diéz...here I come* He nodded. I looked down and away towards my snow cone. I bit into the sugary slush.

One by one all but Rique ran to home base without being tagged. Félix tagged Rique and they walked towards me. Félix then patted me on the shoulder, bent down slightly to meet my eyes.

Wanna play? he asked.

6
THE OLD MAN AT THE CLINIC

Her feet were swollen and the doctor said the baby would come any day now. She served me breakfast, and then laid in her bed with her legs up on a pillow. I buttoned my uniform, almost forgot my bookbag and nearly missed the *autobús*.

That day was just like any other school day at Irene Toland School. Class, then one hour of *volibol*, lunch, then a siesta, then more school, then home. I hopped off the bus and reached papi's grocery. He wasn't there. My father never left the *bodega* unattended.

Miguel the bag boy tried to look busy behind the counter. He looked up.

Your papi ran to the Clínica on Milanés. You have a baby brother. He said for you to go and wait at your abuela's house.

I raced uphill from San Gabriel Street to Milanés and arrived at the clínica, *I want to see my new brother...can you ask mami if it's ok?* My head and shirt were wet. I tasted the salty sweat on my face. I panted. The nurse recognized me, told me she wasn't sure I would be allowed to see my brother just yet, *Wait out front.*

I walked to the terrace. Visitors and families talked with their relatives. All the men smoked. Straddling a wooden *taburete,* I leaned back against the wall and hoped the evening breeze would cool me and blow away the cigar smoke. My pants stuck to the raw leather seat.

Then an old man, I was not familiar with, came onto the terrace and sat across from me. Skinny, his face and arms looked like wrinkled cowhide. He smelled of old person smell. The *viejo* hung his worn straw sombrero on the wrought iron bars on the railing. His faded blue shirt looked mended in at least twenty places. Baggy *pantalones* crumpled at the waist. He tied them with a piece of rope instead of a belt. When he crossed his legs, I saw the balls of his sockless feet through holes on the bottom of one shoe. I wondered why he wore shoes at all, as he looked like they hurt his feet.

What I noticed most about the old man besides his deep wrinkled face were his hands: callused and crooked. Maybe he worked hard with his hands most of his life. But the crippled-looking hands and missing left middle finger did not keep him from lighting a stubby *cohiba.*

In my barrio everybody knew everybody. Being around papi's grocery store all the time, I was not *penoso* about talking with people I didn't know. But I did not recognize this old man, so when he looked at me and asked me why I was at the *clínica,* I spooked.

He uncrossed his legs, leaned forwards and rested his elbows on his knees. Flicking the ash of his cigar at his feet and looking into my eyes, he spoke in a low, husky voice:

Bueyvaca. I live near the water with my son. I don't really know this part of Matanzas. The ambulance...they just brought him here because they thought he might not survive the drive to

Calixto Garcia Hospital. The doctor thinks he has ciguatera poisoning.

The old man asked about me and why I was at the *clínica*, so I told him. He had been an only child and his mother died having his baby brother who died a day after he was born. The *viejo* wished he had a brother and a mother growing up. I didn't care for a grown person to talk about dead babies and mothers. All I could think of was my new little brother.

The old man puffed on his *tabaco*.

I learned to fish from the time I was about your age. My tío taught me to repair nets, catch bait fish, plug holes on the fishing boats with hot tar and clean fish. My aunt taught me to cook and smoke cigars.

When his uncle died the old man, then young, took care of his aunt until she died. He lived in their home and married the housekeeper. The *viejo's* only son, Everto became a bookkeeper and was recently widowed.

The *viejo's* face turned serious. *I fished all my life until two years ago when I was lost at sea for three days. They say they found me tied to the boat, drifting towards Habana, several miles off the coast of Playa Varadero.*

But, how did you get lost at sea? I itched to find out.

After that– my son Everto would not let me go out fishing anymore. His eyes became glossy and he blinked slowly, looking down as if ashamed. *Everto said I was too old for the sea and that it was time that I move in with him.* The *viejo* let out a cloud of cigar smoke in my face. I don't know if it was the smoke or that he made me feel sad, but my eyes got watery. *Lagrimitas?*

I wanted to hear more from the old man, and asked him to tell me more about his fishing. Like any curious seven-year-old, I interrupted him with questions, like what was the biggest fish he caught, did he ever kill a shark, wasn't he scared in the dark with just a kerosene *farol* to light his way out at sea?

I had always hoped to catch the biggest fish anyone had ever caught in Bueyvaca. After sixty-two years of fishing and praying I finally caught a large blue marlin. Hooked him hard with a hand-line on a wood spool and he fought me for almost two days and a night. The old man showed me what looked like healed string burn scars on the palms of his hands.

The *viejo* went into great detail about pulling the line bloodying his hands, how the sun scorched him, how he ran out of fresh drinking water and he was so thirsty he drank his own pee and how he started to see things that weren't there. When the fish first hit the bait, he thought his little skiff would tip and he would go overboard. He prayed to the Virgin of La Caridad de el Cobre, the patron Saint of Cuba and Merciful Saint of all fishermen, for the fish not to break his line.

Sharks circled, and he tied the marlin by the tail and bill to the side of the boat while he tried to row against the current. The winds kicked up and he thought he could see the lighthouse on the Bay of Matanzas but the sheets of rain blinded him, pelting his body. He lost an oar as the waves rose and fell, and the weight of the giant fish tilted the skiff as he was tossed like a rag doll on a merry-go-round. The rudder broke off and all he had left was one oar, which he tied from either gunnel and around which he wrapped both arms with rope. He laid in the bottom of the boat and hoped his back wouldn't break with the pounding of the waves.

The last thing I remembered was the face of the Virgin Mother looking down at me in the darkness, smiling through the rain and wind. I awoke with the sun in my face and heard people talking.

Men in uniform looked down from the deck of a large

motor boat. *Levántenlo con cuidado—make sure he is still alive and check for broken bones*, one shouted.

He said they lifted him onto the large *lancha* with the *Guarda-Costa Cubana* insignia on it. The *viejo* barely lifted his head to look back at his little red and green fishing boat being towed. The tail of the dead marlin, still tied to the side, bobbed in the wake as they headed towards shore. The smell of rotting fish left his nostrils as the *lancha* sped away.

Ricardito? Where have you been? My father stood there, arms crossed as he glared at me. I nearly fell off the *taburete*. The old man looked up at my father, nodded, and took a deep suck on his *cohiba*. He waved his hand for me to step away.

I never forgot what the old man told me on the terrace at the Clínica the day my brother had been born, in the year 1957. I would dream about the sharks and the storms on many nights after that.

Several years later, Mrs. Farley, our 10th grade English teacher in New Jersey had assigned us to read a book by Ernest Hemingway about an old man and a fish. As she collected our book reports from the class, Mrs. Farley raised her eyebrows, and looked towards me,

Well, you are from Cuba, aren't you? ...Did you ever hear of Ernest Hemingway? He spent a great deal of time there. I hesitated and thought about saying, *No, but I think I met the old man who caught the fish.* I nodded instead and handed her my report.

7
THE SIGHT OF BLOOD

The first time I fainted I was six. Mami took me to Dr. Pancorvo the day before because one of my teachers said I had been acting tired and mami thought I looked pale. I was always skinny and everyone said I was a picky eater. When I did eat meat, which wasn't very often, it was either sliced ham, or *croquetas* (ground beef and ham rolled with cornmeal and lightly fried). After examining me, Dr. Pancorvo sent me out of the room so he and my mother could talk.

I didn't much like Dr. Pancorvo. As mami finished speaking with him and closed the door behind her, I knew something was not right. She held a little slip of paper with something written on it and she walked towards me with her eyes looking down.

"*Vamos, Ricardo.*" She rarely called me Ricardo. I was "Ricardito" or "Ricar" to all my family. The serious look on her face told me that this day would not have a good ending. I was right.

That night my mother said nothing about my visit with Dr.

Pancorvo. I asked her to tell me what he said and she changed the subject. I kept asking.

Dr. Pancorvo wants you to have some blood tests tomorrow... but ...it's nothing.

Nothing. Nothing??? I shouted. *What do you mean, blood tests? Porqué? I don't want to... why do I have to have análises de sangre? I'm feeling muy bién! I don't want a blood test.*

She hesitated. All she said was *We'll talk with your father when he comes home.* That is what she said when she meant there would be no more discussion. And there was no more discussion.

I went to bed that night like on most summer nights in Matanzas. It was hot even with the windows open and the fan on the table at full speed. No tropical breeze that night. I got under the mosquito net, pulled a handful of my comic books from beneath the pillow and started reading. But I could not concentrate. All I could think of was "blood tests." I didn't need any blood tests and I wasn't about to get them. My mother came into the room, kissed me *buenas noches* and turned out the lights. That was it.

But I couldn't sleep. Then I realized that the reason mami had been so quiet about the discussion with Dr. Pancorvo must have been Gilberto. My Uncle Gilberto had died two years earlier. He was my father's next to youngest brother and he was thirty-seven when he died. He looked like Clark Gable, the American movie star, and all the years of working on my grandfather's farm had given him muscles that most people envied. Anyhow, my Uncle Gilberto died of a blood disease. I remembered he would come to Matanzas on horseback and they would give him blood transfusions all the time and then he would stop by papi's grocery before he would try to ride back. For a while there I thought it was the blood transfusions that killed him.

I found out years later that it was a disease called leukemia. At that time there was no treatment for it, which is why *tío* Gilberto died and why I think my mother was so worried about my blood. Just as he began to become sick, he would feel and look tired and he got very pale. My mother was worried I looked pale.

I tossed and turned in my bed and started to believe maybe I looked pale, too, and I began to imagine getting all the blood transfusions and dying of a blood disease and how I forever hated Dr. Pancorvo for asking me to have blood tests and blamed my mother for making me do it. A mosquito trapped inside my net kept buzzing near my face as I laid on the pillow. "*Muere, cabrón*!" I slapped it hard when I thought it landed on my face. The buzzing stopped.

Morning came and I was in a panic. When I looked in the mirror, I had dried blood smeared on my cheek and on my hand. I began to wonder if I could get leukemia from mosquitoes. No breakfast.

Whenever you have a blood test you are not supposed to eat. She never told me why that is.

I began to think this was punishment for some bad sin I had done. I didn't know what I had done wrong to deserve this. I really felt weak. Simply walking the three blocks to the corner *laboratorio* on San Gabriel and Compostela streets had me panting. When I saw my reflection on the window, I saw myself maybe looking a little paler, too.

We walked in and mami handed the laboratory lady the slip from Dr. Pancorvo. She looked at it, cleared her throat, looked directly at me, and asked us to take a seat. I begged my mother to take me home. "No *es nada, Ricardito...solo una pinchada de mosquito.*" Just a little pinch, like a mosquito bite, she assured me.

The laboratory lady walked us into a back room. It smelled

of antiseptic smell. She then asked my mother to sit behind me, with me standing up, my back to mami. She instructed my mother to hold out my left arm. The woman leaned forward and wrapped a thick rubber strip around my arm, which pinched when she tied it into a knot. I could smell the cotton ball full of alcohol she held in her hand. Little drops of the cold liquid dropped on my pant's leg and I remembered the smell distinctly. I kept pulling my arm away from the laboratory lady while my mother forced it outwards towards the woman.

The woman said, *I just know you are a little big hombre... this is just a pinch...it isn't going to hurt. It's just like a mosquito bite.* She grabbed the fingers of my outstretched hand and tapped on the crease where the arm bends with her long fingernails.

See? It won't hurt. It's going to feel just like that, she said.

She then turned and reached to unpack a glass syringe from a silver-looking metal tray. At first, all I saw was the metal needle. Then she screwed it onto a large glass syringe. I started sobbing and I felt my heart thumping as it wanted to explode out of my chest. She stuck the needle in my arm. My other fist was clenched so hard and I bit my lip and tried not to cry, until I saw and felt the blood being sucked out of my arm and into the cylinder of the syringe as she pulled on the plunger. I couldn't stop shaking.

Hold still...don't move or I will have to stick you again! I hated the witch in a white dress.

I tried to look away, but I felt the life as it went out of me through that needle into the syringe. I tried to close my eyes but the smell of alcohol and feeling the blood swirl and fill the syringe while my mom held me stiffly and the witch towered over me was more than I could take.

The room felt hot and my head began to float. I could smell

the antiseptic and the alcohol. I felt like someone pulled the floor from under me, as I sank between my mother's knees.

The next thing I knew, the laboratory lady was kneeling beside me. She held a cotton ball-full of alcohol over my nose and my mother was on her knees, on the tile floor of the *laboratorio* on the corner of San Gabriel and Compostela streets. Mami held my legs up in the air, while the laboratory lady said *Take a deep breath...we are finished. You will be all right.*

This all happened in probably less than two minutes. It felt to me like hours. It was like I woke from a *pesadilla*, not sure at first where I was. When the lady in the white dress told me I could sit up, I felt the rubber strip still tight around my arm. Blood dripped from the hole where the needle had been in my arm onto my pants and shoes. A little puddle of blood formed on the tile floor. My mother was speechless, her eyes were big and wide, like she had seen a ghost. I began to think she needed to have some laboratory work done on her, she looked so pale herself. I began to feel light-headed again, but looked away towards the wall and took deep breaths.

After I got cleaned up, mami picked up her purse, paid the lady and took me home. She didn't go to work at her school in Aguacate that day and instead stayed with me at abuela's house. She said nothing the rest of the day, not even after my father came home.

A few days later, Dr. Pancorvo told my mother I was anemic and gave her an iron tonic for me to take. He also told mami to give me a tablespoon of cod liver oil every day. The iron made me constipated and the cod liver oil was awful to swallow, especially after it became rancid in the heat. I was constipated and miserable, but I was ready to do anything for anemia, just knowing that I didn't have Uncle Gilberto's leukemia to worry about after all.

* * *

Four years later: My father had sent me to the dentist on Cuba street. *El Dentista* was one of his good customers and although none of my friends ever went to this dentist, my father said he was a good dentist. I had very bad teeth. Lots of cavities. My father said it was because I didn't drink milk, which was true. I think also it was because I took every opportunity to eat candy from our grocery store, especially the American Bazooka bubble gum, which I constantly chewed while not in school, and which I always kept four or five fresh pieces in my pocket at any one time.

I don't remember the dentist on Cuba Street's name. I think it is a mental block, because like Dr. Pancorvo, I didn't like him either. Doctors and dentists in Cuba were all the same. They never treated kids like people. They always spoke to the parent and not to you and acted like they knew something you didn't know, and whatever it was, it was going to hurt one way or the other.

"*El Dentista*" had a habit of humming to himself. I remembered his dentist's chair, shiny silver like metal and all the instruments of destruction on a white porcelain tray beside the chair. And he had a little machine with pulleys and a motor at the bottom, the one attached to the little wand with the drill. Most of all I remembered the pliers (as I called them, because they looked like Uncle Yayito's pliers that he fixed his car with but these were made of a shiny silver metal instead.)

That afternoon my father walked me to the dentist on Cuba Street and left me with the lady that helped the dentist in the office. I soon found out she was his secretary, his nurse and major torture assistant. She told me to lie back in the chair. I was worse than scared. *El Dentista* then came in and started humming.

Open wide... ahhh. He stuck a wooden thing that looked like a wide popsicle stick in my mouth, then looked around with his light and mirror strapped to his forehead as he hummed his way around my *muelas*.

I have known your father for over ten years. I was one of his first customers, but that was before you were born. Hmm hmm hmmm. He tried to hum the National Hymn of the Republic of Cuba.

Hmm... This does not look good, he turned to his assistant. *We will have to pull this muela, but it won't hurt. Just a pinch... and we are done.*

Just a pinch. Seems to me I had heard that once before when I thought I had a blood disease like my Uncle Gilberto and nearly lost my life at the *laboratorio* on the corner of San Gabriel and Compostela a few years earlier. But I had no choice this time. *Mami* wasn't there and *Papi* left and went back to la *bodega*. I was trapped. The assistant stood over the dentist's shoulder and looked at me while *El Dentista* hummed into my helpless, gaping mouth. His assistant was a pretty lady, very young with dark wavy hair to her shoulders and very red lipstick that made her lips look wet. When she leaned over the dentist to adjust the overhead lamp, I saw the space where her breasts came together and this distracted me. She was really pretty.

El Dentista said he would give me numbing medicine so it wouldn't hurt. When he didn't say anything about a mosquito pinch that scared me even more. Then his assistant handed him a syringe. I wanted to shrink and slide off the chair and run, but I was trapped, and besides I wasn't about to make a fool of myself in front of the dentist's pretty assistant with the red lipstick and nice breasts. I had to be a man and so I tried to act like a man.

As the dentist hummed, I felt him pull on my tooth with

the pliers. He was not gentle. I couldn't feel my tooth but it felt like he was about to break my jaw. Then I felt the pliers slip and heard a crunching sound like a chalk that crumbles when one steps on it. It was like he lost his grip.

In between scrunching his brow and drops of sweat forming on his nose and forehead as he dug inside my mouth *El Dentista* said, *Hmm...it looks like the tooth cracked. I am going to have to make two little cuts on your gum so I can get all of it out.*

He swabbed the inside of my mouth and then pulled out a bloody cotton ball, which he dropped onto the tray in front of me.

Díos mío, this was more than I could stand! My forehead started to feel warm and then cold and then little drops of sweat started to trickle down over my eyebrows. I felt light-headed. The assistant leaned over me and I could smell the perfume on her dress. She patted my forehead with a damp towel and then she said something, I can't remember what, but I think she tried to calm me down, and I felt like there was no way out. I wasn't about to cry or scream. *El Dentista* straightened, straddled his legs over my legs and then leaned over me. I was trapped in his chair and I wasn't about to be a coward in front of the pretty lady who smelled of nice perfume.

He continued to pull with his pliers, twist and humm and I felt like he was about to tear the lower part of my jaw out of its joint. He then pulled harder, gripping, and twisting at the same time, now with two hands. He grunted and stiffened his back. I shut my eyes tightly, bracing for bad. Another crunching sound and then a pop, and I opened my eyes to find his pliers hovered over my face with a piece of foul smelling, bloody tooth in them! Blood was on his pliers and on his hand.

We got it all now. He un-straddled himself off of me and asked Estela, his assistant, to help clean me up. She dabbed my face and lips with a clean wet towel. Blood and blood clots were on the towel. She gave me a glass of salty water to rinse and spit out into a basin. More clots. *El Dentista* stepped out of the room.

I was still light-headed. My jaw was numb and I wondered if *El Dentista* had broken it trying to pull my tooth. Estela helped me off the chair and sat me down in the vestibule, in front of a fan. I thought I had urinated in my pants, but it was all sweat in my crotch and on my buttocks and back. Nervous sweat. Thank God!

I sat there for five minutes or so as I told myself I wasn't going to get dizzy or pass out. But I was dizzy when I tried to stand up and then promptly sat back down. I didn't want Estela to notice. *El Dentista* came out a few minutes later, told Estela to put a wad of gauze in my mouth and for me to bite down and hold it there, which I did, while Estela held her chest against my face, arm over my shoulder which totally distracted me from the waves of dizziness and light-headedness.

Ten minutes or so later, Estela said I could go if I wanted, but I must keep the gauze in between my gums and keep my jaw clenched for a while. I waited for my father but he didn't come. We didn't have a telephone and my father's *bodega* was about four blocks away. I told Estela that I felt better and I could walk home by myself. She smiled and said something to the effect that I was a very courageous young man. I stood up, not wishing to disappoint her. My jaw was busy squeezing a wad of wet gauze in my mouth, so I mumbled that I could walk back to my father's. I tasted blood in my throat.

It was mid-afternoon, very hot, humid, and sunny. I don't remember reaching the corner down from *El Dentista* on Cuba Streets' office. Then I heard someone saying, "*Niño...que pasó? Estás bién?*" I opened my eyes and saw three people stand over me. They looked down as I laid on the street near the grate on the drain ditch by the curb. I had no idea where I was and when I tried to speak, I choked and coughed up a bloody wet gauze. One man recognized me, picked me up in his arms and carried me to my father's grocery store.

That was the second time I fainted. I'm glad that Estela didn't see me.

* * *

A year later came my third major problem with blood. I used to raise chickens with my Uncle Yayo's help. I had five egg-laying hens which were blue/black, stocky and the most beautiful and gentle creatures. I had raised them all as chicks I hatched from fertilized eggs which my uncle had taught me to candle, and which I put into an incubator he built. These five hens were black hens, a breed from England that laid large brown eggs with a very yellow yolk. They were my prize hens, not only because I raised them from the time they hatched, but because all the other kids in the neighborhood envied how pretty they were and to me they were soft gentle pets.

I learned from my uncle, who knew a lot about chickens, that sometimes when chickens ate bad corn (he said sometimes a mold got on the corn) the corn would swell up in their gullet, and would not go past the pouch below the swallow tube. When this happened, the chicken stopped eating and often died. My uncle used to put a little rubber tube with a syringe filled with water down the chicken's beak and flushed the swallowing tube and crop. And sometimes the chunks of grain or other material like balls of grass and straw came out and the animal would be back to normal. If this didn't work, my uncle said the only way to save the chicken was to cut into the crop and pull out the bad corn kernels.

One day, one of my hens got sick. She moped around,

barely walked even when poked at, wouldn't eat or peck, even at the mushy rice I tried to feed her. Uncle Yayo could feel her gullet bulging, full of hard kernels. He tried to flush her gullet but that didn't work and she almost drowned. He told me the bird would die unless he cut the crop open and took out the moldy grain. He tried to do it, but I had to help him because my grandmother did not like him doing this.

I loved my hen. I was ready to do anything to save her life. My Uncle Yayo got some of his instruments from a little wooden cigar box where he kept them and he boiled them. These were used surgical instruments that my uncles, both of whom were doctors in Placetas, had given my Uncle Yayo. Uncle Carlos had taught his brother, Yayo how to stitch and stop bleeding vessels and how to bandage them. My Uncle Yayo could do anything, and most of the time he sewed up any of his animals that got injured, or drained pus boils from them if they got infected.

Uncle Yayo had me straddle a *taburete* (a traditional Cuban wooden chair with goatskin leather seat) in the alleyway of my grandmother's house, beside the water spigot where we had earlier tried to flush the hen out. I held the hen upside down in between my legs and spread my hand over its breast while I held its legs with my other hand. Uncle Yayo knew when chickens were placed on their backs with their head and neck dangling a little, that they almost always seemed to still. They couldn't move, which was what my hen did when I held her.

Uncle Yayo then wet the hen's breast feathers with a cloth soaked in alcohol and clipped several of the feathers, which left a bare skin patch about the size of a peach at the base of the hen's stretched neck. I was surprised when he made a light quick cut with a Gillette razor blade, and how quickly the skin split open with the animal barely noticing. I held my hen firmly but not tightly. He took a couple of little scissor-like clamp instruments and teased the skin apart. He found the gullet and crop of the hen just below where the swallowing tube was. Blood oozed out and he put a gauze on it. Just then I began to feel a little lightheaded and then cool. A cold sweat came over my forehead and back of my neck. My ears rang.

Uncle Yayo called out to my grandmother who was in the house and asked her to get him a bottle of mercurochrome he kept in his medicine cabinet. I did not want my hen to die. I felt ripples inside my stomach, and a sick feeling went from my throat upwards. I fought the lightheadedness. I broke out into more of a sweat. I closed my eyes so I wouldn't see the blood and the cut on my hen's open neck. I heard Uncle Yayo say he got four kernels out, then like in a black tunnel, darkness came on at the same time his voice became harder to hear, like he was in another room. I woke in my grandmother's bed, not 15 feet away. My shirt and pants were wet with water and blood. Abuela said later that I had fainted just as she walked out into the alleyway with the mercurochrome. Minutes earlier, she had seen me shake a little, look dazed and then started to fall forward, over the hen and onto my Uncle Yayo who at the time knelt, while holding a forceps with a needle and thread. As I passed out, I must have fallen forward onto the chicken and my uncle broke my fall. Abuela had lifted me and dragged me into her bedroom and onto her bed. She put my legs on two pillows and a cold wet rag on my face, and then I awoke, not knowing or remembering what had happened or where I was. I was confused.

Uncle Yayo had not finished stitching my hen's neck when I fainted and slumped towards him while I held the chicken in between my legs. After abuela dragged me to her bed, and saw I was awake, she ran to my uncle, picked up the flailing, bloodied chicken. She held it still for my uncle until the last stitch was in. When he dripped mercurochrome onto the stitched area, the hen must have felt the cold, stinging liquid, and jumped out of his hands running wildly into the courtyard.

The hen survived. Since then, I have fainted several times over the years, but never again during surgery, through medical school or during four decades in my medical career. What is it about the sight of blood that starts such a reaction in humans? It must be a purely human reflex, as much as I have looked, I have yet to see or read about any other animal faint at the sight of blood.

8
THE BEND IN THE RIVER

My friend Juanito's father's farm was about 100 acres of cow grass and trees, and a river came down and around the hills above his property. His father always said that the rich soil and having the river run through his farm was the best for grass and for fruit trees to grow. And he was right. There were oranges, tangerines, papayas, keneps, mango trees, and guava trees, most of which grew wild by the river and roads on the farm.

Whenever I visited Juanito I made sure I took at least one or two old socks full of steel ball bearings which I had rescued from Chucho's garage. Some were the size of small marbles, others were smaller. Ball bearings made great ammunition for our slingshots. The larger ones were best for shooting close up, but the smaller ones were good for shooting mangos or papayas off trees, at kites, or at street lamps, at palm trees or at lightning rods on top of houses because they traveled farther. We shot at anything that wasn't alive.

One weekend Juanito and I used up most of our bearings by Friday afternoon shooting at old cans and glass jars we set up against the wall of the barn to practice our aim. Juanito said he didn't want to use his glass marbles, and I wasn't about to use what few bearings I had left.

Why don't we go to the river in the morning to collect nice, round stone pebbles?

Juanito said he had discovered a big bend on a part of the river where there was a big pile of small round stones on a little island in the middle. But his father had told him to stay away from that area and not to jump the barbed wire fence that had red rags tied to it because it was a very dangerous part of the river.

Why did your papi say it was peligroso? I asked him.

Juanito shrugged his shoulders. He never said why his dad said it was dangerous.

Don't be a cobarde, Ricar. We both know how to swim and besides we have our slingshots, so nothing to be afraid of. Vamos a explorar.

I followed Juanito. About 100 yards on the edge of a large pasture we saw a barbed wire fence. The red rags were tied to the bottom wire instead of the top wire which I thought was weird, because people in the pasture would not see them, especially when the grass was high. The fence was also different than most cow fences because it had four barbed wires instead of three. We followed the fence until it turned to the left and under the trees and down across a real narrow part of the river. We walked over a fallen tree at that part. It was just like a perfect bridge. Where the fence crossed the water, there were branches and sticks that must have gotten stuck on the wires from when the river got high during rainstorms. The water looked deep in that narrow spot and the current must have been kind of strong because a stick floating in the water moved fast below us. We crossed the river and on the other side followed the fence through some trees. We climbed up a lower branch of one of the trees and jumped over the fence and back towards the direction of the river. Sure enough, there was a clearing and a big sunny bend where the sun shone on hundreds of round rocks of all sizes.

I told you this was a great spot for pebbles!

To get to the pebbles, we had to go in the water, which on that bank looked shallow and the current was slow. We waded in, about knee deep, for about twenty or thirty feet before we reached the pebble mound. We filled about 10 old socks each with mostly round, smooth river stones. We were on our knees, in the hot sun, busily picking the best pebbles. The breeze and sound of the current around the bend drowned out all other sounds so that sometimes I couldn't hear Juanito talk even if he was just a few feet away. The sun felt good, and my jeans and sneakers had begun to dry as I knelt on the pebble hill. It smelled good to be out in the fresh air.

Hey, do you want to pick some guavas?

I had noticed a large tree growing off the opposite side of the river from where we waded in. The branches of the tree hung down to the water, heavy with fruit. When guavas are green they are hard, and they tasted crunchy and had a reddish-tan pulp which was a little lemony. As they ripened, the skin turned yellow and scraped off easily. The inside of the fruit was soft, reddish, and lemony-sweet. Ripe guavas give off a very sweet perfume-like smell. The smell of guavas in the breeze made me want to reach for the large fruit which hung over the bank of the river.

Juanito and I stood up from the pebble mound, leaving our old socks full of pebbles and our slingshots. We walked towards the large guava tree. The water under the tree was dark in the shade and looked black-green and smooth. Juanito locked the fingers of both hands like making a horse stirrup and as he started to hoist me up to a large branch full of guavas, we heard a low, grunting sound come from under the shadows of the tree.

Hear that? What is it?

Before I figured out what the noise was, something splashed in the water, and pebbles slid, like some animal scrambled on the rocks. A loud squeal almost made me pee in my pants. Then a huge wild pig came from under the tree and ran at us, sinking its legs in the river stones as it headed towards Juanito. I stood with one foot perched on his hands. I reached up and grabbed a branch above my head, pulled myself up, lifted my legs to my chest—I don't know how I did it. I swung over the dark water to the short bend of the river towards the base of the guava's trunk. I saw and heard Juanito run the other way, screaming "*Ay Ay Ay Ay, que me mata!*" (it's gonna kill me!)

The wild pig was black, probably at least two-hundred pounds, with two large curled *colmillos* that stuck out of each side of its lower jaw. The beast looked furious. The animal's large balls dangled from his crotch, swinging side to side in between his back legs as it headed for Juanito, and it almost tripped over its balls as it ran over the river stones at full speed.

Juanito jumped in the water as the pig followed him. I jumped off the trunk of the tree. Juanito was but thirty feet from me as he tried to run for the other side of the river and slipped in the water. I reached down to find a rock on the bank but all I could find around the tree where I stood were guavas! I was not about to jump in the water again. I was so desperate that I picked up a rotten guava and flung it at the boar. It got the pig's attention, because he whipped his thick ugly head around and grabbed the fruit with its mouth. By this time, I pulled some rock-hard green guavas off the branches above me and threw them at the hog as hard as I could. A couple hit it on the head, but instead of scaring it, the animal got wilder, changed direction, and came squealing back onto the pebble island, heading for me at full speed.

Juanito must have reached the other side of the river because I could hear him running through the trees. I did the same from my side and tripped a few times, going through the thick *manigua* pushing aside the low branches and thorny vines along the way. I finally got out of the woods and saw the fence with the red rags ahead of me. I heard noises in the bushes behind me as the squealing got closer and closer. The boar was coming for me. I didn't look back, but ran as fast as I could towards the fence. I headed for a wide fence post, put both hands on top of it, and I don't know how I jumped the fence, but before I realized it, I was on the pasture side. I kept running. I stepped and tripped into a mud hole, and lost one sneaker, but just kept running. Four or five cows ahead of me ran off when they saw me coming. I slipped on a fresh cow patty and landed on my butt. I got up and kept running. I saw Juanito in the distance across the pasture near the trees below the house. He had stopped, had his hands on both knees, and his head down, huffing. I caught up to him. My butt and thigh were gooey with wet cow shit.

What happened to you? He said, looking at me real weird.

What do you think, what happened? The pig happened! I think I was more mad than scared, and my lungs hurt because I breathed so hard.

No, I mean that! How did you get that? Juanito pointed at my face.

I swiped my forehead and noticed my palm was red with blood mixed with fresh cow shit, mud and sweat. My arms looked like someone had sliced me up with a knife and the sweat made all the scratches sting. I leaned up against the trunk of a large *zapote* tree and tried to catch my breath.

You know what?

What? I said, looking back over my shoulder.

We left our slingshots and ammunition at the river.

We went in the back door of the house so nobody would see us, washed up and put on clean clothes.

Time to eat...wash your hands and help set the table. Juanito's mom called us twice.

I sat down at the table and tried to hide my scratched-up forearms and hands underneath.

Dios mío! She looked at me horrified. *Where did you get all those scratches? Here...let me take a look...*

I guess there was no way to hide the scratches on my face and upper arms. By this time Juanito's father came to the table and sat down. He looked at me, then at Juanito, real slow-like, but said nothing.

I... I was just running through some bushes and got scraped up a little.

A little? My goodness, it looked like you had a fight with a cat, you are so scratched up! How did you get so cut up? Did you boys have a fight? She looked at Juanito, who looked down at the table, trying to avoid the question. I shook my head and then looked down also.

Juanito's father then said in a very matter of fact way, *I guess you boys went down by the river to get pebbles...is that* right? We looked at each other and nodded. *And I suppose you went down by the big bend, where the fence with the red rags are... and where I told you not to go?* We nodded again. He said nothing, picked up his fork and continued eating.

Let me guess. You jumped the fence and went to the river there. Juanito looked at me and then at his dad. He knew. I was so mad at myself for listening to Juanito. I was also very embarrassed. Juanito's father was a good friend and long-time customer in my father's grocery.

You are lucky you didn't get ripped apart and eaten, he said.

I hope you learned your lesson. He scooped some black beans and poured them over his rice.

The nutty smell of those beans steaming over the rice is making me really hungry, I said to Juanito's mother, hoping to change the topic, but to no avail. Juanito would just not let this go.

But papi, that animal almost killed us. And if we hadn't left our slingshots there I would have killed it myself, I swear! Juanito looked at me, then at his mom. *I'm going to go back and kill it-you just watch!*

You will do no such thing, hijo. You went into his territory and the animal was just trying to defend itself. Plus, you disobeyed me. He looked at both of us and then motioned to his wife.

There is some mertiolato in the medicine cabinet. Those scratches could use some tending to.

Juanito's mother dabbed *mertiolato* all over my arms and face. *Mertiolato* was like red alcohol but smelled different and was less liquidy. It was what everyone used at home to keep cuts from getting infected. When she was done, I looked like a clown, painted up with red splotches everywhere I had a scratch. It stung real bad and I wanted to cry but I tried to be brave and besides I wanted to make sure Juanito's mom and dad would let me come back and visit again so I had to be good. But I was ashamed. Besides, I just knew when mami found out what happened and saw me all cut up she would be very upset, and worst yet, papi would spank me and then probably never let me visit my friend again-ever. That night I awoke in a panic. The boar was biting my arms and face after it had eaten my left foot and my sneaker. I touched my face and felt the scratches and cuts, but my face was still there. I reached for my left leg and feet. No sneaker, but all five toes were there.

9
PEELING BACK THE BURLAP

The night before, I had helped Uncle Yayo dab the rooster's cuts with vaseline to keep the mosquitoes away. The bird's puffy eyelids looked like they hurt, showing bloodshot skinny slits for eyes. A three-inch long cut looked raw and swollen. A row of the stitches Tío Yayo put in went from the bird's neck, down and across its breast.

The bird lay no closer than three or four feet from any of the other cocks in the yard. That was how far the roosters were tied by a leg to keep them from fighting each other. All the others clucked and crowed as they flapped their wings expecting their morning food. But this one lay on the ground, not moving. The only way I could tell it was alive was when his chest moved up and down a little, and his beak opened and closed as it tried to breathe. What was left of the fleshy part on top of his head was now swollen and purplish looking. Smaller fresh cuts and little stab holes which I guessed were from the other animal's spurs covered his head and neck.

Uncle Yayo cleaned the rooster's water bowl and filled it

with fresh water from the hose. He also did this for the other eight warriors, who kept scratching and pecking at the dirt in their tied-down places around my grandmother's yard. He then fed each two handfuls of hard corn mixed with grit. The cocks pecked like they were in a hurry to eat, cleaning up most of the grain-all except for the one which just lay there, on the dirt.

Uncle Yayo squatted and lifted the wounded cock, then tucked it under his left arm. The animal didn't struggle. With the fingers of his left hand, he opened the bird's beak and with an eyedropper in his right hand, filled from the bowl and dripped fresh water into the cock's beak. The animal seemed to blink as it swallowed. Two dropperfuls. Then two more. He lay the bird back on the loose dirt. No corn or grit. He placed a fresh leaf of lettuce on the ground beside the cock's head.

Mami called from the kitchen window, *Es tarde, Yayo, we need to get to Aguacate!*

They would be late to their classrooms that morning and my mother could do nothing about it because she didn't drive and it was Uncle Yayo's car. She was used to this. She was the school principal, and of the four instructors in the little country school they ran, he was her best teacher. Uncle Yayo finished feeding the cocks. The sleeve of his suit coat was smudged with dirt and bloody goop mixed with vaseline. He hosed the birds with a fine spray till they dripped wet. The birds acted like they liked this. He rinsed his hands.

By now the morning sun came up over the mango tree in the backyard. The wet roosters looked so beautiful in the sun, especially their shining blue-green tail feathers. Tío Yayo gave the hurt rooster another leaf of lettuce. The cock lifted its head, rolled, then stood, wobbly-like, and tried to peck down towards the lettuce but with those puffy eyes I don't think it saw well. A dark green liquidy poop squirted from his behind onto the dirt and the bird paced a little, then shook his feathers and wings a little. It laid down again.

Ricardito, make sure you move him towards the shade after he dries.

Uncle Yayo stood up and took the car keys out of his pocket. The jingling sound spooked the rest of the gallos finos. My school bus would be at the corner of *calles* Medio and San Gabriel in twenty minutes.

"*Gallos finos*" as fighting cocks were called, were bred to be like gladiators. Most people who knew anything about fighting cocks knew that these birds should never be kept in cages or with other animals as they would likely ruin their feathers and peck or poke with their spurs or beaks through the mesh till they either got all cut up, or worse yet died trying to escape or fight each other. Only someone who didn't know anything about *gallos finos* would let more than one male bird loose in the same open space without risking one or both getting hurt or killed. My grandfather said it was important to start tethering the roosters since the time they became young cockerels, so the animals were used to the tethers in the yard by the time they became full grown.

It seemed like Uncle Yayo had a special bond with animals. During the feeding and cleaning two times a day, he went around doing this real quiet, like one does when one goes to church. The birds seemed to know him and never in all the years of my *gallo fino* experience did I ever see any of the birds attack him. One day my uncle was sick in bed and my abuela took me along to do the feeding. As I bent down to pour corn from the feed can, I must have surprised the bird. In an instant, the cock ruffled its neck feathers, took a little step back, then with wings flapping and spurs in the air, it jumped forward and carved two bloody cuts in my arm. My grandmother then got into it with a flying shoe, much to the gallo's wishing it hadn't hurt me.

Abuela didn't hide the fact taht she did not like cock fighting. As I got older, I found out she liked the birds well enough, but hated the idea of them being allowed to hurt or kill each other for "sport" just because it was a macho thing men did. But I learned that like people expected of every good, loyal Cuban wife, my grandmother never criticized her *marido*, my abuelo. Although people in the streets and even Manolito's father, the policeman said it was against the law. Next to baseball and boxing, it seemed like everyone in Cuba had cockfights. As an eight-year-old, I wasn't sure what to believe.

Although Tío Yayo did most of the feeding and care of the roosters, they actually belonged to my grandfather. I realized years later, that like abuela, Tío Yayo did not care for cock fighting either. But he cared for animals. I don't remember him ever going to the fights. But it would be my uncle who doctored the birds whenever they got sick or hurt, like when they got mosquito pox, or worse yet, when he had to fix cuts and bleeding holes on Sundays after the fights.

I remembered dreading when abuelo came into the house on Sunday afternoons from the cock fights, especially if he came back with burlap bags tucked under his arms. Although he never said it, from the time I was as little as I can remember, I was expected to act like a man, and that included me being there to greet him when he came home from the cockfights. I could tell Sundays caused great nervousness in my uncle but for me, it was a sickening feeling that I had to hide. Sometimes Uncle Yayo untied the twine around the mouth of the bag and peeled back the burlap, only to find the dead and limp-but-still-warm, bloody body of yet another lost bird. It was expected of me to pull the spur wraps off, wash, and save the spurs, then wrap the animal back in the burlap, and bury it in the garden. I always said an Ave Maria for the dead birds even though all the kids in the barrio said animals had no souls-but, just in case, I did anyway.

Whenever one of his cocks died in a fight, my grandfather, very macho as he was, always got very serious. It wasn't like he was mad. Like the priest at a funeral, he in a deep respectful voice spoke about the strength and courage of "*El Chucho*," or of "*Gavilán*," names he gave his fighting roosters. He usually said something about the animal like *He was the toughest and most loyal gallo fino I have ever had.* But sometimes he said under his breath things like, *Ese bastardo Romero, played dirty on me and put poison on my cock.* He wouldn't think I heard these things but I did. I didn't always understand what he meant.

I never saw abuelo act like he seemed sorry, look sad or cry whenever one of his cocks died. But Tío Yayo would always be quiet and sad-like when he took care of the hurt birds. He treated them like mami did when I got hurt, real gentle. When they laid there shivering and all cut up, he patched their cuts like he was a real veterinarian. Although he was only a teacher, he taught himself from reading books about diseases of animals and from my uncles who were surgeons he learned how to sew up and treat cuts. They gave him used surgery instruments. Uncle Yayo used alcohol and mercurochrome to treat the wounds and he boiled the instruments before he used them.

I always heard grown people say that kids learned from what they saw not from what others told them to do and think. I adored and respected my uncle. Same with abuelo. I begged Uncle Yayo for a little fighting cock for myself. After all, many of the kids in the neighborhood had them, as did abuelo. My grandfather would have none of this. *The cocks are not toys, they are not pets.* It was a sport for grownups only.

Several weeks passed. One day after returning from the school where he taught in Aguacate, my uncle pulled his Chevrolet in front of abuela's house. Signaling for me to go to the back of his parked car, he pointed to a spot on the street, just off the curb and told me to stand there. I thought this would be just another twenty minutes of guarding his car while it was parked on the street. Instead, he leaned towards the trunk and inserted the key in the lock. *Close your eyes and put your hands out*, he directed. I heard the trunk pop open. He placed what felt like a basket in my hands. Before he let me open my eyes, the basket bobbled like there was something alive inside it. I almost dropped it. There was a smelly stink. Then I heard a clucking sound and felt a wriggling.

I opened my eyes. In the basket was a burlap bag with a little white Bantam fighting cock inside. His feathers were scraggly, some were bent and others broken. The bantam only had one good eye, and many scars on his comb. Chicken poop was smeared on his tail feathers and wings. One of the toes in his left leg was missing, like it had been cut off.

Don't say anything to Papá, where you got this rooster...you hear me? Uncle Yayo pointed his finger at me.

As a boy, that was a great defining day for me. I didn't realize then that I had not only been given a great gift, but a responsibility. Tío Yayo expected that I would be in charge of this little ugly rooster. If he died, it would be my fault. If my grandfather opposed my keeping it, it would be my problem to fix. It was also a great message I received: that I was trusted by my uncle (who rarely trusted anyone), and more importantly, that he trusted me with a life, because he loved animals so much.

It would be my job to accept an ugly and imperfect-looking animal with gladness. It would be my blessing to groom it and care for it. Years later I would come to appreciate that most things that have really meant anything to me were like this little pathetic rooster, given to me as imperfect and usually showed up when I least expected.

I discovered that inside the bony body of my little Bantam was a ruthless warrior. No sooner did I carry it from the car into the yard where all the other fighting cocks were, he leaped out of my hands and with spurs flying ahead of him, the little guy charged viciously, and landed atop one of my grandfather's prize cocks. We had to wrap a burlap bag around the bantam, as my uncle pulled the larger fighting bird by his tethered leg while I received several cuts on my arms and face in the struggle to separate the tangled birds.

Gauging from all his battle scars, little "Fosforito" (aka "The Igniter") as I named him, must have been a veteran of many fights. My uncle said his hoarse-sounding crowing was probably because he might have had his throat damaged in some fight. He pointed out to me a long deep scar just under Fosforito's beak, with ragged tissue healed over his neck.

For over two weeks I had to move slowly around it and throw bits of food before the Bantam before it let me come near it without attacking me. I fed the little guy lettuce and corn and little chunks of *boniato*. He eventually let me touch him, then pick him up from the tether and hold him without pecking at me. I trimmed his broken feathers and greased his crusty, peeling legs with olive oil. I fed him ripe guavas, misted him with water every morning and gave him plenty of sunshine. Over the next several weeks he started to gain weight, his feathers looked glossy and pearly white, and I took him out on the street to show him to my friends. Several of them had beautiful Bantams of many colors that they raised or that their parents bought for them. Their birds made my little guy look pathetic. My Bantam didn't look as nice, but to me he was a great fighter.

Then one Sunday afternoon, after having to say a second Ave Maria in abuela's garden, I laid the shovel down. I decided then that Fosforito would never fight another rooster. I would still help abuelo and Uncle Yayo with feeding and even on Sunday afternoons if they insisted. But only because I had to.

10
THE HOT WATER BOTTLE

My grandmother had an amazing ability to heal. I was convinced she could cure any illness, and neighbors and friends of our family always sought out her many home *remedios*. I used to have spells of horrible stomach cramps for which Dr. Pancorvo instructed my mother to give me paregoric drops. I did not care for paregoric, for even though I liked the way it tasted, after I took it, it always made me feel strange and groggy, and like I was going out of my body. Besides, seeing things that weren't really there when I took that medicine always terrified me. That was what the paregoric did to me.

I learned years later that paregoric is a concentrated tincture of opium, highly addictive and potentially lethal. I am sure my mother had no idea that Dr. Pancorvo had directed mami to feed me opium. Was Dr. Pancorvo trying to kill me? Since my mother was generally away teaching school, and my grandmother was not particularly fond of medicines, during those times when my cramps grabbed me, abuela out her magic water bottle instead. Years later when I was grown up, abuela told me she didn't much care for Dr. Pancorvo, either.

Abuela placed tap water into one of the big pots she hung from the ceiling hooks in her kitchen. Then she'd put a handful of charcoal from the pail she kept outside the door into the stone charcoal grill pit. She crumpled up a sheet of old newspaper and lit it with a match. When the charcoal started to burn, she heated up the water. She dipped her index finger into the pot from time to time, just to make sure it was hot enough, but not scalding.

When my cramps were tolerable, I sat on a wood crate in the corner of the kitchen and watched Abuela go through the water-heating ritual in wonderment. Sometimes the pain was more than I could stand, and I started to cry and walked around doubled over. She moved me over to her bed in the room beside the kitchen where she knew I could hear her and she me. I can still remember the soothing gurgling sound of the hot water as she poured it into the red rubber bottle—the sound a thirsty person makes when they chug a large drink. With a towel, she put a special strangle hold around the neck of the bottle, held the neck just so, ensured the hot water never spilled as she poured it in. I could see the dense steam column condense as she screwed the top on and tested the flank of the flat red rubber bag against the skin of her face.

There is power in that bottle, I thought as I watched her.

Within seconds, she squared my hips flat on the bed, looked directly into my eyes.

Here, hold the bolsa with two hands, keep it very still on your belly. Try not to move so the water inside the bolsa doesn't slosh. And breathe despacito.

Abuela then sat on the edge of the bed with her knees together. She placed the palm of her hand softly on my shoulder. Her wire-rimmed glasses encircled her brown eyes which made them look big and round and kindly looking, like those of a cow. She looked down, almost like she started to pray and then she told me stories.

Ricar, have you seen how little birds sit together on top of the electric wires on the street when it rains? Why do you think they do that?

I don't know, abuela. Why?

I don't know, either. She would chuckle.

Without fail, and within minutes, I was like in a dream, all kinds of quiet and peaceful, and the waves of cramps would ease as I balanced that water bottle on my belly and she continued her stories in a soft, soothing voice. My eyes got heavy during these water-bottle-balancing acts, but unlike when I took the paregoric, I didn't feel weird or see things that weren't there. Sometimes I woke and found that I had fallen asleep for one or two hours and hadn't even noticed this. By this time the cramps were gone, and the water bottle, which had usually slid off the bed onto the stone floor in the bedroom, was no longer warm. I might hear Abuela in the kitchen and I felt completely back to normal and ready to go out and play with my friends or feed the animals before my Uncle Yayo came home. Sometimes I felt so good she made me warm sweet lemonade with fresh squeezed lemons she picked from the lemon tree by the kitchen.

My grandmother died when she was 96. Every night before she went to bed, she insisted on drinking a tepid glass of water with two tablespoons of sugar dissolved in it. I don't know whether this is why she lived so long. I do know that she was a major reason I became a doctor and that from her I learned the meaning of good bedside manners and of caring.

I suffered through Dr Pancorvo as a kid. I am sure that his intentions were good, but in retrospect, I don't believe he was a very kind person from the way he treated people, especially when they were sick. He was gruff and came across as uncaring. In contrast, I so much trusted my abuela's hands-on approach whenever I became sick, that her holistic demeanor prompted me years later to want to be a doctor. I do have Dr. Pancorvo to thank for making me become the kind of doctor he was not.

Years later I wondered what must have gone through my young daughters' minds when suffering through bellyaches as they were growing up. I heated the water in the microwave just-so, and choked that red rubber bottle with a towel, poured the steaming water without a spill, and used all the healing magic that abuela passed onto me on them. I have often wondered if they really believed my stories about the little birds sitting on the wires in the rain like I did.

11
OH-EH, OH-EH... OH-EH, OH AHH

A marching band? They couldn't even afford to buy paper for school in Aguacate. But someone had given my Uncle Yayo a dented, green-tarnished brass *corneta*. My mother thought a marching band was a brilliant idea. But no teachers in the school had any musical training whatsoever. There was no reason to start a marching band for their fledgling school in the middle of rural nowhere, but the *corneta* planted a seed.

Weeks later my mother heard someone in our neighborhood in Matanzas wanted to get rid of a pair of *timbales*. She picked them up. Then Tío Yayo found two dented cymbals in some mechanic's garage junk pile. He fashioned leather straps for them and shined them up along with the tarnished *corneta*. Two teaspoons of salt and white vinegar in an empty bottle of Coca Cola, shake, soak, and rub hard. The green tarnish disappeared. The idea for a marching band evolved. Word got out.

Mami bought a used snare drum and a base drum. A farmer in Aguacate donated a cowbell and a neighbor gave Tío a triangle. Tío made the batons for the *timbales* and the bass drum mallet out of *majagua* wood and wrapped cowhide. The *corneta* would provide the melody. An old man in Aguacate was a trumpet player and he would teach his sixth grader grandson three melodies on the *corneta:* The National Hymn of Cuba, and two other "marching" tunes. That was it.

The marching band would be by default percussion-heavy and un-uniformed. They would repurpose the Cuban flag from the flagpole in front of the school for marching in the *desfiles*. Tío made a flag carrier harness out of an old belt and a wooden cup he covered in leather. Abuela sewed colorful triangled banners for the marchers. Three marching tunes, repeated over and over and over again, and they marched and banged away, undisciplined, but with fire in their bellies.

After much begging and groveling, I got to be a "guest" member of the *Escuela Primaria de Aguacate* marching band. The reason? There was a kid in my neighborhood in Matanzas who was a whizz on the snare drum in their school marching band and mami was friends with his mom. She asked him to teach me some basics. I was thrilled. I don't recall his real name, because everybody in the *barrio*, including his family, called him *El bizco* (cross-eyes). He could play, rumbled, and buzzed those wires at the bottom of the tight *drum*, at times his play was like thunder in a barrel and at others, he could sound like a housefly flittering inside a paper bag.

Oye, Ricar, éstos palos son para ti.

El bizco gave me a spare set of drumsticks, said they were mine to keep. They were chipped, but *so what? Tío* sandpapered and shellacked them. In retrospect, I think mami regretted letting me do the snare drum thing. I snared every waking minute, so much so she couldn't take it anymore and sent me to practice over at abuela's house. When I did, abuelo's fighting cocks, the peacocks, the birds, and the dogs crowed, cackled, or howled. Tío's monkey would screech and became frenzied if he even saw me carrying the snare near the courtyard. Abuelo wasn't happy about my noise, either, but Tío Yayo was thrilled with my progress and he finally let me join the marching band. But my practice was limited to tapping on a wooden cigar box while at abuela's.

Mami and Tío thought it would be great to have a "hymn section" so about six kids from the school who had memorized the National Hymn of Cuba were the singers. No ability to sing was required, just enthusiasm and desire to show up, sing louder than the drums and march at the same time.

Al combate corred, Bayameses, (Run to battle, "Bayameses" natives of Bayamo)

Que la patria os comtempla orgullosa, (Your country looks upon you with pride,)

No temais una muerte gloriosa, (Never fear a glorious death,)

Que morir por la patria es vivir (For to die for your country is to live...)

Eventually, a much-needed drum major was added. She was outfitted with a blood-red beret (the figurative heroine in a famous Cuban depiction representing Liberty), and a blue cape made by a seamstress in Aguacate, a white blouse, red skirt and a *batuta* (drum major baton). A beautiful full-faced girl with shiny cheeks and plump calves was the leader of the *Escuela Primaria de Aguacate Marching Band.* She didn't know music, but could march and pump the *batuta* up and down and side to side like there was no tomorrow. Nose up in the air, head cocked, she blew *el silbato* draped around her neck with a most authoritative staccato, heralding stops, starts, or changing marching tunes for the ragtag phalanx of twenty or so schoolkids that trailed her in semi-orderly *desfile.* That was the marching band.

Every *Dia de Independencia* or formal holiday was celebrated with the *Escuela Primaria de Aguacate* band marching through town with parents clapping, mangy dogs barking, roosters crowing in front yards and little children hopping excitedly, rattling cans with pebbles in them and following the band through the dirt streets of the town. It was like *a comparsa* not unlike those seen in the streets where marchers and dancers *arroyaban,* strolling to the beat of their various musical instruments every year before Lent during *Los Carnavales.* Who would imagine this marching band would bring such joy and unity to the town of Aguacate? Mami and Tío.

Mami and Tío's idea would become an informally formalized school *endeavor.* What started out as a marching band became a daily routine in the school yard. Kids on their own started their own percussive "sessions" and now the *Escuela Primaria de Aguacate* had an unofficial "music class" midmorning twice a week during *recreo.* And why not? Cubans for the longest time have been blessed with the Afro Cuban tradition of *conga, bongó, batá* drums, *guira* (gourd), *quijada* (donkey jawbone with loosened teeth that rattled), *maracas, claves* and the Spanish infusion of *castañuelas,* The music making gave the kids a creative way to let off steam.

Every city, village, town, hamlet, sugar plantation in Cuba was full of gifted street-corner musicians, mostly self-taught and unschooled in tablatures or such. Drumming was a primarily male activity and kids learned what they heard their uncles, fathers and grandfathers play on the street or in *bembé* gatherings. It was on the street corners and alleys of Cuba that the *rumba* was born. *Santería,* an Afro-Cuban religion prevalent in Habana and Matanzas provinces was also rich with African music tradition. *Santero Orisha* dieties, a morph of Catholic saints and Yoruban gods and goddesses were assigned specific percussive rhythms or *toques.* These infectíously mesmerizing rhythms echoed in just about every corner of every town, or rumbled from back yards where *bembés* were held, invoking followers to join in the *prahkatá páh, prahkatá poom-paddáh, poom-paddáh* as their *tumbas,* percussive mantras for the beckoning of the spirits, rattled the chests of the dancers and players, and rumbled on for hours on end.

Most Cubans know that when they hear, *Oh Eh, Oh Eh, Oh Eh, Oh Ahh...* eventually, the rhythm is bound to get them. To this day, I remember every *toque El bizco* taught me with great precision. Every now and then I am tempted to roll two sticks on the bottom of a trash can and imagine myself marching down the streets of Aguacate like it was just yesterday.

12

VENCEREMOS!

It was my summer vacation and I didn't want to go. But mami and tío Yayo insisted. She tried to bribe me and packed a *merienda* in a brown paper bag with a guava paste and cheese sandwich, and a ripe mango. Even that wasn't going to work. I was not happy. She had to push me into the back seat of the car.

We have to teach the people. Fidel says so.

It was 1961. On the way past the town of Aguacate, I sat in the back seat beside a stack of booklets, notebooks, and a roll of sharpened pencils. The booklets looked like the comic books my uncles would buy me whenever they came to visit. Only these were printed on brown paper bag with red and black colored letters and cartoons of grownups holding rakes, hammers, and machetes. At 11 years old I read and wrote very well. The words *compañeros* and *solidaridad, campesinos* and *el future, venceremos* and *el trabajo* were not like the words in my reading books, nothing about *See Pablo run. Juana loves her dog.* But while I knew some of those big words: "*Colleagues,*" *"farmers," "the future," "we shall conquer,"* and *"work."* I didn't understand what *"solidaridad"* meant.

Tio drove along an uneven red dirt road full of muddy ruts. I saw him act ticked that his car got splashed with mud. I smelled pig shit in the air as we drove by a field and when I looked out the window, I saw two pigs grunt under the shade of their *cochinero* near the road. Tio sped up to get past the awful stink, hit a big rut and muddy water splashed inside the car. He was really mad now. We pulled over and *tío* insisted we had to get out and walk; that he didn't want to get his car stuck in the mud. As we got closer to a farm, two mangy dogs barked at the gate. Instead of hinges, the rickety gate had rope loops tied to posts.

A curious boy came running to us. The dogs followed him. The boy must have been around 4 or 5 years old. Barefoot, he wore a small unbuttoned white shirt which was no longer white. He had stringy hair, a dirty face, and hands, and he was covered with mosquito bites and scratches. His little fingernails were black with dirt and he had snot coming out of his nose. He had very skinny arms and legs and a very funny-looking, swollen belly with a pooched-out belly button the size of an egg. Mami said his swollen belly was probably from infection with *parasitos*.

Mami called out, *Señora! Señora? Soy la maestra, Lydia Silva de González.*

Out of the palm-roofed hut came an older woman whose hands were shriveled. She wore men's shoes with no socks, but she might as well have been barefoot because I noticed the holes, especially the one shoe which looked like someone had cut off the front part, where two twisted toes stuck out.

Llamo a mi hijo, said the woman. *Paco!!! Paaa-co!* She turned towards a small shack next to their *bohío* where a man splashed his face in what looked like a water trough for animals.

Paco, la maestra y otro señor. My Uncle Yayo introduced mami and himself as teachers. Tío asked about the name of the people in the farm down the road, and proceeded to cut through on foot carrying booklets, pencils, and notebooks while mami and I stayed.

Hands dripped, Paco stepped away from the trough and walked toward us. He had several missing teeth, was very thin but very friendly, probably in his thirties, but looked much older, like poor people with hard lives look. Mami said she was there to teach the adults in the family to read and write and it wouldn't cost them anything, that Fidel Castro was paying for it. Paco dried his hands on his pants and took a book. I think this was probably the first time in his life that he had held a book. The way he opened it, I knew he couldn't read because he held it with the writing upside down. Brown paper from used magazines and paper bags were a luxury for poor people because they didn't have money for toilet paper. I wondered what Paco thought with that book in his hands.

Mami pulled me behind her. The mangy dogs barked without stopping but kept wagging their tails. *Silencio!* the old lady shouted, and the dogs immediately quieted. We went inside the *bohío.* The palm roof was still wet from rain from the night before. It smelled musty and wet inside but the dirt floors looked swept. I also smelled burned turpentine. Crickets chirped on the inside part of the roof. Two *faroles* hung from posts. That must have been the only lights they had at night, because there was no electricity like in our house in Matanzas. Four *hamacas* hung from the posts inside, and I think that was where the family slept because I didn't see any beds. A chair was in the corner with a piss-pot under it. No other furniture, not even a mirror. We walked through the *bohío* to the backyard where two orange trees shaded handmade benches with a very rough looking table beside the benches. A pipe with a pump came up from the ground and a tin bucket hung from a hook on the spigot. We sat in the shade and mami started to explain to Paco, his wife, and the older woman with the holes in her shoes about how to learn to read. She gave them each a small notebook, pencils, and erasers.

Vámos a leer y a escribir.

The pipe with the pump leaked and I heard the plop-plop of water drip into the bucket. A chicken pecked at the moist ground beside the bucket. I sat on one of the benches and watched mami. She was like a magician. In a few minutes the three adults had their heads buried in the booklets. She told them about the letters of el *alfabeto* and that putting letters next to each other made words. Then she wrote their names in the front of every notebook and pointed to what she wrote.

Here. That says "Paco," your name.

The man's eyes got real big and he smiled. I thought it was strange that she had to teach them how to hold a pencil. We spent probably two hours there that morning, maybe longer. After a while it got boring just watching them, but then this monster rooster grabbed a hen's comb in its beak and tried to hump the hen by the fence. The hen jumped up on the fence and got away. But on the fence, there were beautiful *estropajo* vines growing on it. The vines were full of gourds and yellow flowers. *Estropajo* was the name of a plant that grew on a vine and the gourds when you dried them out in the sun left a stringy ball of fibers, and this is what people used as a scrubbing tool for bathing or for washing dishes and pots and pans in their houses. I asked the old lady if I could pull a couple of dried *estropajos* off the vine. She nodded and smiled.

The old woman offered us *limonada,* which I really wanted, but for which mami said, *No gracias.* She pretended we were running late and had to leave to teach other families. I think she said no because she wasn't sure about us drinking their water and getting *parasitos*. Paco's wife insisted on giving us a bag with oranges, *boniatos* and two brown chicken eggs. Mami thanked them. I figured mami felt bad about taking what little food they had, but that she did not want to insult them. Mami said we would come back three times a week for the rest of the summer. I stuffed as many *estropajos* as I could in my pants' pockets. I didn't like eggs but mami said I had to carry them anyway. She carried the sweet potatoes and oranges.

Tío Yayo waved us toward his car and he looked unhappy and hot. We walked down the road and out of the gate with the dogs following us. Mami didn't seem to like dogs. I don't know if she didn't like them jumping up on her or if she was afraid. But the old woman called out to the dogs and they left us alone. I remembered getting in the car, eager to eat my *merienda* in the back seat. Nothing beats a good guava paste and cheese sandwich—except maybe a nice, ripe fresh mango.

Es la batalla contra analfabetismo, mami said.

She said analfabetismo means, "when one doesn't know how to read or write." They taught three mornings a week for the whole summer. I was glad that they didn't always take me with them and that I stayed with abuela and abuelo or in Papi's grocery store on some days because all the talk of *compañeros* and *venceremos* got pretty boring and I already had enough *estropajos* at home.

Mami taught three families that summer, and Tio Yayo another three. I was surprised that by the end of the summer, most of the adults could recognize and write all the letters of the alphabet and write their own names and read other words in the booklet. It was like magic. They seemed so happy about it. They started calling us "*Compañeros*" and whenever we were about to leave, they waved and shouted, *Viva Cuba!*

When the lessons ended, I had less than two weeks left of summer vacation and begged mami to take me to Buey Vaca beach. On the way there, one day I noticed new painted signs on the seawalls and along the highway with the words of "*Cuba sí, Yanqui no!*" "*Venceremos!*" "*Labor es victoria!*" Just like in the booklets.

When we got to the beach there was a fat man by a food cart. On the side of the cart was a painted red sign, "*Churros.*" He sat in the shade under a sea grape tree. As I got closer, I noticed he read a booklet and right away recognized the brown pages with black and red print and cartoons. I handed him 10 *centavos.* He handed me a nice, warm *churro.* Looking up at him and with as serious a face as I could put on I said, *Muchas gracias, compañero!* He looked at me surprised, and waved his booklet above his head, he replied, *Viva Cuba! Venceremos!*

13
CAKE SOLDIERS

Señor Calvo dropped a used flashbulb to the floor and as it landed, it reminded me of when airplanes drop bombs on television. Mami had invited my friends from the *barrio* and others. She dressed me in knickers, a short sleeve shirt, and tied a maroon *corbata* around my collar. She combed my hair, sprayed me with *agua violeta* cologne and ordered me to "*No toques*" until Señor Calvo finished taking pictures. The fat man posed me on a chair behind a cake shaped like a fort. I felt his wet smelly breath on my neck. *Hold still*, he said, then walked around and stood in front of me. The flash blinded me but I still made out the brown plastic toy soldiers stuck in the frosting. The cake was lit with five candles. A little Cuban paper flag sat on top of the little tower on the cake. The smoke from Señor Calvo's cigar made my eyes sting, but I stood still.

Señor Calvo took eight or ten more pictures. After he left, I saved the burned-out flashbulbs. I thought my soldiers could use them for future wars. Then I got distracted by the smell of the fresh-squeezed *limonada* my mother had put on the table beside the cake.

My friends sang me *Felíz Cumpleaños*. We ate yellow cake and licked the frosting off the soldiers. We played pin-the-tail on the burro. After everyone went home, I rinsed my sticky soldiers with water in a tin can my abuela kept in the courtyard. I laid them all out to dry in the sun.

Those soldiers became one of my most favorite toys. Some days I made them fight in a war in the dirt piles of the backyard. When I ordered, my soldiers rolled ball bearings I kept from Chucho's garage. They made perfect cannon balls. To get them ready for battle, I used skinny rope from papi's grocery to make little bridges between chairs in abuela's living room. On make-believe farm play days I made my soldiers become farmers and had them stack red kidney beans I took from abuela's burlap bag. These were my make-believe watermelons. I made them load toothpicks from abuelo's desk onto my make-believe card-board-box wagons and took them to my electric train station. I gave the toy soldiers all names and kept them in a little wooden cigar box under my bed. There were twelve of them. I counted them each night before going to bed and placed them in a special order inside the cigar box.

Some years later, as I began to notice little curly hairs sprout from my crotch and painful red bumps pop on my face, it seemed like the soldiers became less and less a part of my days. Catia, the girl who lived on #25 San Gabriel smiled when I passed by her house and I began to notice her legs. I also became interested in playing marbles, making bows and arrows, and I bragged to my friends that my uncle had given me the responsibility of being his assistant in caring for all his birds and strange animals, including a squirrel monkey. Sometimes I missed my soldiers. I would check under the bed from time to time, and over the years, despite some having lost arms and legs, and some missing in action, the unit of my soldiers stayed safe inside my cigar box.

Then one day, on April 17, 1961 the Bay of Pigs happened. The *milicianos* paraded their prisoners like cattle in army trucks, up the main street in Matanzas, and past papi's grocery. The men inside the trucks looked pitiful. Hands and feet muddied and full of dried blood, they were tied with ropes, they sat on the trucks, looking down, like they were ashamed for people to look at them. Many had weepy, bloody cuts and scratches, and all were full of mosquito bites and sunburn. I overheard mami and papi say that many soldiers were killed and many more were caught in the swamps. That night, Che Guevara spoke on the radio and said they were "*Traidores de la Revolución.*"

Two years later, my family and I were at the José Martí Airport in Havana waiting on a flight to Mexico. I had never been on a plane. I heard my parents talk about how we were "refugees." I took my favorite *soldado* out of my back pocket and tucked it in the palm of my hand, hoping I might take him with me. But at the last minute as mami went to take me by the hand, she panicked and told me to leave it behind. (Exiting *refugiados* were not allowed by the *milicia* to take toys or other luxuries out of the country.) I was afraid if the human *soldados* at the airport caught me with my toy *soldado*, they might think I was stealing, and they might make me stay behind. So there I left him, my cake soldier, in the basin of the water fountain. Minutes later, the bearded men in green fatigues, wearing black berets, and black and red armbands frisked me and my family. When satisfied, they let us board the Cubana Airlines *aeroplano* out of Havana. I wanted to go back to the water fountain for a rescue, but mami's desperate grip on my shoulder hurt, as she dragged me towards the plane. She acted very nervous and scared, so I walked beside her.

Several years later during a class discussion in the Ivy League University I attended in the United States, a classmate praised President Kennedy's bold actions on the Bay of Pigs. But to many people, and especially to Cubans who had lived through it, and for many American military involved in the planning, the Bay of Pigs invasion, originally intended as a CIA —backed mission of trained Cuban expatriates who would assault the island to free the country from Castro's regime was one of the most shameful episodes of betrayal in United States and Cuban history. Shortly after the covert operation was launched, President Kennedy at the last minute, ordered withdrawal of American military air and naval backup as the liberation forces landed on the waters of the island. Without backup, the invasion failed miserably. Kennedy believed the United States would save face by deflecting involvement. Many of the liberators died overwhelmed by the Cuban artillery, many others were captured, tortured and imprisoned. The Cuban system under Castro persevered and the failed invasion became a David-against-Goliath propaganda event, with Cuba shaming the United States for decades to follow.

My classmates in the ivy-clad halls could not know that I had been there, that April of 1961, not sixty miles from the Zapata swamp at the time it all happened. Of course, probably none of them heard Ché Guevara on the radio, talking about "*the traidores*." But I did. The pathetic faces of the prisoners on those trucks in Matanzas flashed in front of me. I stayed silent as the discussion continued. I thought of Señor Calvo and the flash bulbs popping in my face, and of the cake soldier I abandoned in the basin of the drinking fountain at the Habana airport on the day I left. I was suddenly overcome by an illogical sense of guilt and betrayal. My bones shook and my skin prickled. I never knew one could feel guilt, anger, and cowardice at the same time. My visceral reaction must not have been subtle, because the students and the professor looked up at me puzzled. I said nothing. Then I pushed away from the table, bolted out of my chair, and scurried outside the class, out of the building, and into the snowy quadrangle.

14
CUCA LA MUDA

No one in Dr. Moorfi's house ever spoke about Cuca. She was Oscar and Rique's aunt, the only sister their mother, Mita had. I guessed Cuca was much older than Oscar and Rique's Uncle Samuel and Mita, but none of us knew how old she was. She was short and skinny like a twig of *caña brava* bamboo and her skin was thin like wax paper, so the blue veins stuck out on her arms and neck. Her yellow skinny legs looked like chicken legs, waxy and scaly. She had a thin face with pointy cheekbones and no eyebrows. Her hair was in *trenzas*, braided like a piece of rope coiled on top of her head. It was the same color as the white hair under her arms. She always wore thin sleeveless dresses with hip pockets and old lady-type socks and these hung half down her bony legs and past her knees. I thought this was because her legs were so skinny. I also thought she didn't have the money to buy nylon ones like her sister Mita because Cuca wasn't married to a doctor like her sister.

People who came to Dr. Moorfi's often thought Cuca was the maid. She answered the door if she saw someone's shadow through the glass, then she would back away and let the person in with a wave of her hand and then ran to the back of the house to find someone, then just like that, she would disappear... *al carajo!* Cuca kept busy either cleaning things around the house or folding things. She kept a square little rag she cut out of an old bed sheet and when not in one of her hip pockets, she put it on her lap and folded and unfolded it, back and forth, back and forth. Sometimes she got into this *manía* and went on for a good twenty minutes at a time. Jorge poked her shoulder and screamed *—Cuca, Que coño haces...what the hell are you doing that for?—* Even when she saw his lips move, she acted like Jorge wasn't even there. She looked down at her rag hankie, patted and smoothed the edges on each corner, then undid what she folded, then she did it again, like the priests do after cleaning the wine cup during *comuníon.*

Although I knew she didn't talk, *La muda* as everyone called her, must have had something else wrong with her. Sometimes I asked her questions and she looked at me like I thought she knew what I said, but she didn't, really. Sometimes, though, I thought when she saw my lips, she either nodded like she knew, or swung her head from side to side, like this let me know she didn't like what I said. If one said or did something which upset her, she peeped real loud— *Abbah...Abbah...pa pa pa pa pa Abbah...—* Félix and Jorge said she was retarded. Rique said she had a brain infection when she was a baby and almost died. *Mami* said Cuca had the *sarampíon* (rubella) when she was little and that Mita had told her she was never the same after that.

Nobody in Dr. Moorfi's family ever talked about Cuca. There was definitely something wrong with *la vieja,* but I think from the way the Moorfis acted, no one was supposed to ask questions. Cuca hardly ever went out of the Moorfi house. She sat in the yard, or swept the front entrance, but she never went out in public, like going shopping to the La Plaza market or to my Papi's grocery or even to church like normal people. Jorge said he thought it was because the Moorfis were afraid if she tried to cross the street and couldn't hear the tram or cars coming, she would be hit and get killed. Félix said it was because the Moorfis were ashamed and because Rique and Oscar's Uncle Samuel was a politician and that if people knew he had a retarded, deaf and stupid sister it would not help him get votes, even when he paid people. I thought it was a little of all these things and more, because Mita would never take Cuca places like sisters are supposed to, and whenever people would visit, Mita seemed embarrassed but at the same time sad to have her sister be there. I always thought it was a shame that adults think eleven-year-olds don't notice these things.

Dr. Moorfi was a bone specialist and his office was in his house. We found out that Cuca spent a lot of time in a room on the second floor. The upstairs of the house did not look like anyone lived there and was more like a place where Dr. Moorfi kept his casting materials and various bone doctoring things like crutches and braces with funny shoes for the kids with *poliomielítis*. Eyebolts with pulleys and chains and hooks hung from the beams in the ceiling. A small door was by the wood steps going to a room which Rique said was where Cuca took naps. She always kept the door locked so we could never see what was in the room, although it looked more like a closet than a room. I never really knew whether this room had a window or even whether she had a regular bedroom downstairs in the main house.

One day, Rique looked up towards the roof on the front of the house, while standing outside by the street. Rique said, —*Mira, this looks like it...see, up there, the round window half open with the pigeon sitting on the frame?...*— he pointed towards the second story of the house around where we thought Cuca slept.

Since most houses in Cuba had no air conditioning, we wondered how anyone could have stayed in that room with no air moving. Rique once stood in front of Cuca so he made sure she could see his lips. He popped her forehead with his palm, *—Tia, mira, how can you sleep up there with all the stink from the pigeon shit??—* Cuca didn't react, she looked down and walked off into the house.

Cuca was like one of those tic-toc little machines that piano teachers use to make you keep the beat. It seemed like she never stopped rocking and moving, even when she took her siesta on the couch near the kitchen. Oscar and Rique had great fun teasing Cuca all the time. They hid her mop or locked her in the bathroom downstairs and held the doorknob tight from the outside, just so they could hear her squeal *—Abbah...Abbah...pa pa pa pa...Abbah...—* Jorge and Félix thought this was really funny, and they always pushed Rique to play pranks on Cuca just to hear her squeak.

Cuca got really mad sometimes. Whenever Oscar or Rique teased her, it didn't take much for her to bring the broom down on their butts. Sometimes she threw a dish rag or empty cardboard box at them, like she meant to hurt them but not really... I'm not saying that Oscar and Rique did not deserve a real whooping, because if I had done the kinds of things they did to her in front of *Papi*, being disrespectful like that to an old lady, he would have had his belt on my *nalgas* in no time. The thing was that Rique and Oscar loved Cuca's "weirdness," and I have to say, Félix and Jorge and I also sometimes acted like a pack of animals and treated her badly. Sometimes even Dr. Moorfi got mad at Cuca and he screamed at her so that the freckles on his cheeks seemed to want to pop out of his face, and he then turned red and shook all over. If Mita was nearby and she heard Dr. Moorfi yelling at Cuca she would run and stand in front of her like a *gallina* protecting her chicks, *—Déjenla tran-*

quila...leave her be, she doesn't comprende what you want...— Dr. Moorfi would walk off, squeezing his hands so tight till his knuckles were white, chin tucked down with his head nodding from one side to another. Cuca then disappeared for hours. We guessed she would lock herself in her upstairs room, often skipping eating and not show herself until we came from our houses to play at the Moorfis the next morning.

Most of the time Cuca stayed to herself. I think she liked washing towels and taking baskets of wet clothes up the stairs past her little room on the second floor, and up the wood steps that led to the *azotea roof*, which was flat and had an iron banister on all sides. On the roof there was a lightning rod with an old torn kite hanging from a string that was stuck near the top of the rod. The kite flopped around like a caught fish in the wind. There were two other poles for hanging a clothesline. Cuca took the wet laundry and hung it with clothespins to dry in the sun. I sometimes snuck up behind her and watched her while she hung clothes. It seemed that this was the only time when she looked calm and even acted like she was a happy and normal person. She would at times hold the damp towels in between her two hands and put her face and nose up to the clean cloth, like she held and kissed a baby. Or she closed her eyes and took deep breaths like she was smelling a flower. When dry, she took down each piece of clothing and folded each like she did with her little square rag, pressing the corners flat with her hands and then placed each piece neatly in the basket, even the socks and Dr. Moorfi's underwear.

One day Oscar, Rique, Jorge and I were washing Dr. Moorfi's Chrysler in the driveway. Cuca walked up by the side of the house. Oscar aimed the water hose at her face and chest —*Time for a bath, vieja!*— We could see her bra and underpanties beneath her wet dress. Cuca went hysterical. She picked up a tin bucket half full of soapy water and flung it at Oscar, and the bucket hit him on the shoulder, and then hit the fender of Dr. Moorfi's car. Luckily, neither the car nor Oscar were hurt and Cuca ran off dripping like a wet cat. We all laughed uncontrollably at Oscar. He looked so stupid standing there wet and soaped up! But by the look in his eyes, he was worse than pissed off, he was beyond *encabronado!*

Hija 'e puta, maldita!— screamed Oscar, *—Damned daughter of a whore that you are!!!*— (Cuca of course didn't read his lips and Oscar, poor bastard, didn't realize he had just called his own grandmother a *puta*!!) I wanted to protest, but being the skinniest, youngest, and smallest of the group, I was scared, as usual, that Oscar and Félix would beat up on me, so I said nothing.

The next day we sat up on the roof of Oscar and Rique's house, playing dominoes, and chewing Bazooka bubble gum, which I took from my father's grocery store. Jorge said *—Oye... this American chewing gum has little funny cartoons inside the wrapper! Félix, what does it say in English?*— Félix looked like his usual stupid self. He didn't read English, he only knew to say *—How ar' jew?* and— *Jew make me laff...* But that was all the *Inglich* he knew, which was all he learned from *los Americanos* that came to Varadero beach... Anyhow, we were playing dominoes, drinking Coca Cola and chewing Bazooka bubble gum when Oscar told us how he would get back at Cuca. He made a noose from a piece he cut off the clothesline, put it around Rique's neck and had Rique go downstairs to the second-floor storage room.

—Rique—, he said, *—keep this around your neck and lie on the floor like you are dead...right in front of Cuca's door—*

Rique lay down outside her door, with the rope tied around his neck, next to a footstool which Oscar made look like it had fallen on its side. Oscar then cut part of the noose end of the rope and made it look like it had torn, and another cut end he tied from the ceiling beam to make it look like Rique had stepped off the stool and then his weight was too much and the rope snapped and he fell to the floor and died.

The rest of us hid behind the boxes of plaster and bandages in the storage area and then waited for Cuca to open her door. Rique had a mouthful of Coca Cola and Oscar told him to wait until he heard Cuca open her door, at which time he slowly let the Coca Cola drip out of the side of his mouth onto the floor. I guess he wanted it to make it look like Rique puked after his neck snapped.

Oscar thought it was a great plan. Jorge and Félix bobbed their heads like those toy baseball player *muñequitos* on the dashboard of cars...they always agreed with Oscar, because I think even though they were bigger than me, they were afraid of him too... Rique, who was the biggest and most macho of the group was quick to volunteer because whenever there was any daring, Rique always had to be it! We waited for almost fifteen minutes, after we realized that it wouldn't matter how much noise we made or how hard we knocked on her door or made "falling" noises by her room. After all, Cuca was retarded and deaf as a doorknob, so she probably wouldn't notice.

Cuca finally opened her door and as she stepped forward, she almost tripped over Rique, faking like he was dead. His head laid in a puddle of brown liquid, his tongue stuck out from his mouth, his body twisted in a weird position that didn't look human. Seeing Rique, Cuca jolted back into her room, like a cat who was about to step on a snake. Cuca's eyes bulged out of her face and she threw her hands up on her head and began — *Abba...Appah...pa pa...pa pa pa...!!*— She shook her head real hard then fell on her knees at Rique's side. She shook him and tried to loosen the *cuerda* from his stiff neck. Rique bolted from the floor, spit and snorted Coca Cola then dropped back down, now really like he was dead.

Cuca buried her head in her hands. She could not look at Rique. Her bones and ribs showed through her cotton dress. She sobbed and put her head down on her thighs, kneeling on the puddle of Coca Cola, her old lady socks soaked the liquid up. She took deep breaths and snorted and sobbed. She couldn't control herself. She just rocked back and forth, seeing her nephew not moving. Félix and Jorge and Oscar howled. Rique stood up and started dancing around Cuca making faces and tugging at his noose as he twirled.

I don't know if there is a word to say how one feels when anger and pity crash with each other. I came hard from behind the boxes, head first at Rique. I felt my neck crack as the top of my head hit the lower part of Rique's back and he flew across the room into Cuca's door. His face smashed into the wood frame.

—Ayyy coño, damn it!!! Maricón, you faggot! Rique screamed.

I dropped to my knees and put my arms around Cuca. I remember the way she felt under me as she shivered there. It was like the feeling I once had when I caught a bird with a broken wing in my hand. Cuca shook like she couldn't control herself, then she stopped shaking.... stopped moving.

I cannot remember whether Dr. Moorfi or Mita heard my screams for help. Cuca could not read my lips.

15
THE UNFORTUNATE KIMBUMBA INCIDENT

Generoso never played with us in el barrio. Maybe it was because we never thought of inviting him, or maybe because he acted like he would not have fun playing hide-and-go-seek or *kimbumba*. I think it was probably a little of both of these things and of his being shy, besides being very uncoordinated and not liking to sweat. Or maybe it was just that his mother forbade it.

Call me Gene, (pronounced Henneh) he would say. *Not Generoso.* That was the name his parents gave him.

Gene was the pretty boy in Matanzas Oeste. He was thin, had shiny brown curls and pearly pink skin. He had freckles on his face, arms, and even on his legs. Instead of walking like most people, he flitted, holding his hands at his sides pointing away from his hips, his spider-like fingers spread apart like they were wet and he was airdrying them. When he walked, his neck stuck out, with his nose pointed up, like he was a little prince. People would mutter, *There goes the little pargo...*

Generoso's mother was a seamstress and her family lived next door to Ezequiel the *Polaco,* who ran an upholstery and materials shop out of his house. They shared customers. His mother made Gene pastel-colored gingham short sleeve shirts and knickers which she sewed herself, as she also made all the clothing her family wore. She insisted Gene button the top button of his shirt collar, even at the worst of summer, which we thought was strange.

Although he may have acted like a sissy most of the time, I always had the feeling Gene wasn't like people in the barrio said he was. The truth is that I couldn't figure out if Gene was really a *pargo* or if his mother had taught him to act the way he did. Mami told me Generoso's mother had wanted badly to have a daughter. But his mom almost died from bleeding while giving birth to Gene, so her husband decided they would have no more children. Generoso's father worked at night and was hardly around so probably all Gene ever learned was to walk and act girly from his mother.

Ay, Princesa...que bella, mi niña preciosa, my precious little girl!

Generoso's mother owned a little brown Pekingese, named Princesa, which like Gene, she would pamper. She never let that dog be a dog. I think Gene's mother saw Princesa as the daughter she never had. It seemed like every day the dog had a different colored *cinta* tied in a bow to the hair in between her ears. Gene's mother made his father install a knee-high wooden gate with slats in the frame of the front door so that Princesa could poke her little wet nose in between the rungs and have a view of the street without escaping.

Gene got the daughters of his mothers' customers to play hopscotch with him when they came for fittings, which is why me, Vento, Jorge, Oscar, Rique, Félix, Manolito, and even his little brother Pepito found ways to play street games in front of Gene's house, which was across the street from my abuela's house. There were always girls there, lots of pretty ones, too.

We didn't want to talk with the girls back then, but we wanted them to talk about us.

One day we played *kimbumbu* in front of Generoso's mother's house. *Kimbumba* was a popular street game played by most kids in Cuba. My grandfather told me it was invented by slaves. I think this is probably true, because the word "*kimbumba*" sounded like many common African-Cuban words, including "*quimbombó*," which is the word we used for "okra."

Kimbumba could be played by two or more players just about anywhere. The *kimbumba* itself was a wooden stick, about as long as the palm of my hand and as thick as a broomstick, and both ends were shaved down to as thick as my thumb. The batter, held a foot-long wooden stick as thick as of a broomstick, would hit a pointy end of the *kimbumba*, and it would flip in the air, up to about a foot or foot and a half in height, depending on how good the batter was. With the *kimbumba* in the air, the batter hit it towards the fielders as far and hard as he could.

Kids spent many hours playing *kimbumba* in the neighborhoods of Matanzas. The game was fun, but dangerous. A flying *kimbumba* or bat could poke your eye or break your nose or bruise a shirtless chest or arms or legs. We played the game "*a mano limpia*" (with bare hands). Wearing gloves took the macho out of it. It was an unwritten rule in our barrio that if you didn't play *kimbumba a mano limpia*, you could always sit on the curb and watch the game with Princesa and Generoso.

One hot afternoon, in the middle of a tough *kimbumba* game, it was Félix's turn at bat. It had rained a couple of hours before and steam rose off the hot pavement, which was still wet. It was like little rainbows floated over the street. Margarita, a very pretty *mulata* who lived on Calle Río played hopscotch with Gene on his sidewalk. She wore a light blue *blusa* and her wavy chocolate braids went down to her waist. Félix, who liked Margarita, wanted her to get his attention.

Princesa laid down, sprawled, and panting on the cool tile floor of Generoso's mother's front door. Her little snout hung over the rungs of the gate. Félix popped the *kimbumba* into the air, and as it tumbled, he pulled back on his bat, shouting *Margarita, para tí...un Hon Rón!* (Margarita, a home run, for you!). The sharp clapping sound of wood on wood when the bat hit the *kimbumba* startled everyone.

Seconds later, everyone heard Princesa yelp like someone killed her. Little Princesa became the unintended victim of Félix's flying stick. The poor little bitch had splintered *kimbumba* stuck in its snout. Gene threw his head, arms, and skinny fingers up in the air and began screaming hysterical-like *M-A-A-A-mi, MAA-A-mi, mataron a Princesa!!!* (Mommy, mommy...they killed Princesa!). Margarita joined, *AY-AY-AAY...la pobre perrita! Hijos de puta!* ("The poor little bitch... you bastards!")

When she heard the people's screams and the dog squealing, Generoso's mother clip-clopped in her *chancletas* down the hall. She couldn't stop when she got to Princesa. Her thick legs tripped on themselves and she kicked the gate onto the dog. Princesa was trapped beneath the gate. The boys scattered, knowing how nasty Gene's mother could be. There was no time to run across the street and hide in abuela's house.

Without thinking, I slid on my knees onto the tiled entryway. Squarely in-between Generoso's mother's fat thighs, I dove beneath her skirt. I scrambled to grab Princesa's back legs, and while I held the dog, Félix slipped around Gene's mother's big *nalgas*, lifting her skirt, then the gate off the little dog.

In a quick move, Félix pressed Princesa's head with the palm of his hand against the floor, and pulled the splintered kimbumba from the dog's nose. The *perrita* snarled, but the yelps stopped instantly. The panic of the moment must have caused someone to lose intestinal gas. I don't know if it was Gene's mother or the little Pekingese. Generoso's mother then screamed at me,

You indecent disgusting boy, get out from under my saya! which made me feel relieved, because between the odor and with what I saw looking up in between that woman's legs I was more than glad to crawl away.

Gene was hysterical. Sweat dripped from his face onto his pretty lavender shirt. He sobbed by the window, hands curled over his eyes. I walked over, and I put my arm over his shoulder. I told him it wasn't his fault. I felt bad for him, knowing his *mamá* would surely blame him for leaving Princesa unattended and that his father would probably give him a whipping later.

Margarita winked at Félix. Generoso's mother stood on the sidewalk, fuming. She held Princesa in her large flabby arms as the little dog's badly cut snout bloodied her perfumed, talcum-powdered bosom. Those of us who stayed at the *kimbumba* accident scene (Vento, Jorge and Rique had already disappeared) were warned by la *mamá* that if we ever dared play *kimbumba* in front of her casa again, she would throw boiling water on us, then call la *policía*.

The following week I received an envelope with my name on it. In it was an invitation to Gene's birthday party.

16
RETRIBUTION

Vento and Oscar said not to go. Of the boys in our barrio, I think only Manolito, Pepe and I were invited. My mother said that unless I was sick, it was not nice to not go when one is invited to something. I didn't think I would be sick the next week, and after my mother bought a gift for me to bring to Gene's party, I couldn't see getting out of it, other than catching some infection or breaking my leg at the last minute.

Mami said I needed to wear a nice shirt to the party and that I had to wear leather shoes and not my sneakers. This really got me, because it was summer and during vacation all I wore were my favorite canvas shoes called "Keds" which mami bought for me at the Woolworth American store whenever she went to Habana to visit Uncle Migue.

The day of the party came. My abuela ironed my favorite white and maroon plaid shirt which she had made for me. I wore this shirt with white linen pants and my brown leather lace-up shoes. I was hot and sweating. What kind of playing could one do in white pants? I started to think Vento was right, but I walked out of my abuela's house and took the gift across the street to Generoso's birthday party, still hoping I might catch an infection so I wouldn't have to go to the party.

As I got to the door, I heard laughing and the radio playing inside. There were lots of girls' voices and howling laughter. Generoso's mother opened the door before I could knock.

Hola, Ricardito, the party is in the yard.

She took my gift and put it on the table with the others. Little Princesa growled and then yipped at me as I entered through the sewing room. I wondered if the dog remembered that I held her down the week before while Félix yanked the kimbumba out of her snout. She had a crusty scab on her nose. The dog followed me to the yard, growling. When I got there, I was mad. I was surrounded by 12 or 13 girls, all shouting and laughing. No one noticed me standing there. I saw no other boys there, until I heard Manolito's voice behind me.

It's just you and me and Pepito with the sissy birthday boy here...the rest are all hens. grumbled Manolito.

When I saw him and Pepito I was happy for more than one reason. I was glad I wouldn't be the only other boy beside Generoso at the party and also because Manolito's mother made Manolito wear *bombaches* (mid-calf pants with elastic at the legs) with high socks and yes...leather shoes! I felt like at least I had regular long pants, even if they were white, but at least they were not stupid-looking *bombaches.*

We drank *limonada* and ate sweet yellow cake with white frosting. That's what every birthday cake was made of in Matanzas. Then we sang *Feliz Cumpleaños* to Gene and it was like a wedding. He jumped around, arms up in the air, twirling in the yard, with all the girls clapping and cheering for him. For almost the first hour, Gene never even came close to us boys or spoke to us, although he knew we were there all right-he looked our way, smiled, threw his head up in the air and walked the other way. Margarita sat next to him, getting Gene's full attention. I was glad Félix was not at this party because he would have been jealous and would have probably punched Generoso in the nose.

Generoso's mother hung the *piñata* from one of the low branches of the large mango tree in their yard. One of the girls had a broomstick and after two strong whacks, she ripped the blue paper horse's belly in two. I wondered just then if this girl might want to play street kimbumba with us some time—she had a strong batting arm. I pulled a nice ripe small mango off one of the lower branches and ate it. I couldn't help it.

As the insides of the blue *piñata* emptied onto the flagstone floor of the patio, all the kids scrambled to pick up candy. Manolito and Pepe got down on their knees and were like scooping machines, stuffing their pockets full of *cariocas* and little boxes of *chiclets*. I did not want to get my white pants dirty so after rinsing the mango juice off my hands, I bent over to pick up candy. In the crowd of girly bodies smelling of violet water and the swirling of skirts and hair ribbons, someone pinched my butt real hard. It did not feel like a girl's pinch and it hurt like hell. I figured that most girls at eight or ten would not dare pinch a boy's butt, and certainly not that hard. Since Manolito and Pepito were in front of me when it happened, I decided there could only be one other person to blame for the ass-pinching. And it was not Generoso's mother.

In Cuba most boys are taught that there are two bad things a man does not do to another man: You don't call someone's mother a whore and you don't pinch another man's ass. I don't think anyone besides whoever it was that pinched my buttock and me had noticed what had happened, that's what I first thought. But I could not take the chance on suffering the humiliation that anyone would have seen another boy pinch my *nalgas*, especially in front of a bunch of girls.

I backed out of the group around the *piñata* and sat on a

chair by the garden. As I looked across the crowd, Gene was nowhere to be found. *Cabrón*! My blood boiled. I needed revenge. Vento was right after all. Generoso was a mean and tricky sissy-mamma's boy. Meanwhile, Princesa laid down on the patio floor, stared at me, snarled, white teeth on pink gums showed...just watched me.

We moved to the living room where Generoso's mother had pushed the furniture up against the walls and she had pulled up the curtains in the doorway between the living room and her sewing room, letting the breeze come through from the patio. On one wall was a thick cardboard cut-out of a donkey. It was painted grey with tempera paint and both ears were black, like the furry cloth strip that Generoso's mother held in her hand, with a small red tack at one end.

Who wants to be the first to pin the tail on the burro? his mother said.

Margarita jumped forward as she took the tail in her hand. Generoso's mother blindfolded Margarita and spun her around. After a few turns and some wobbly steps, Margarita stumbled a little, arms reached out in the air, searching. That was when I got a great idea. She eventually pinned the tail on the donkey's nose and everyone, including Generoso laughed real hard and clapped.

Who wants to be next? said Gene's mother. I jumped, hand up in the air. I had my plan.

Generoso's mother put the blindfold on me and spun me around. When she let go, I got on my knees until the dizzy feeling eased up and I found my balance. I didn't care about my white linen pants anymore. I began to imagine the room in my head, listening for the various voices giving me directions. I kept listening for Gene's girly voice and tried to imagine where in the room he was. As everybody shouted, I moved real slow on all fours, closer and closer to where I heard his voice, but ever so sneaky and careful. I was somewhere between wherever everyone told me the donkey was and where Gene's voice was. I thought Gene couldn't be but 2 or 3 feet from me. Picking up the black cloth strip with the tack in my right hand and acting as if I headed in the direction of the donkey, I suddenly turned to the sound of his voice and shot forward with all my strength, fully intending to knock over Generoso on his freckly, pasty face.

As I shot forward with all my might, I hit what felt like either a piece of furniture or a door. Some of the girls screamed and I felt pain and at the same time I touched my nose and felt it click like my nose bone was broken. Whatever my face hit, it was real hard, and I fell on my hands and knees, head down. A warm, sticky liquid dripped from my nose to the back of my hand and down my arm. My lip felt like it was swelling. I exploded, I was so mad. I stood up, ripped the blindfold off my face and there was Generoso, just smirking. He stood a couple of feet just on the other side of the little wooden gate on the threshold that his mother used to keep Princesa from leaving the house. The gate was smeared with blood-my blood. Blood on my face, on my nose, on my favorite maroon and white shirt. Blood all over my white pants.

Everyone laughed and made me feel stupid. I started to feel dizzy when I saw all the blood, but I must have been so mad, I didn't even think about fainting.

You are going to pay for this, you little spoiled maricón!

Revenge is not sweet. One always pays to get it and acting on something while one gets mad always comes with a price. I suspect to this day, if Generoso is still alive, wherever he is, that his recollection of this event would be more satisfying to him than it has been to me.

17
ON THE BAY OF MATANZAS

It was Félix's idea to take Oscar and Rique's uncle's rowboat, and then go out into the middle of the bay. I had just turned eleven and we were out of school for summer. Oscar and Rique's Uncle Samuel was a local politician with friends who from time to time gave him gifts, like this boat, in return for doing things.

The rowboat was nothing special-12 feet long, flat bottom, made out of wood, with two bench seats. Samuel kept the boat tied to the bank across the street from the house of a lady who wasn't his wife. It was by a small dock downriver from the La Plaza *mercado*, about two blocks past the San Juan Bridge as the river entered the mouth of Matanzas bay. Oscar and Rique's uncle hardly ever used the rowboat and his lady-friend wouldn't go in it because she couldn't swim. Félix found out that the lock around the chain on the dock wasn't really locked, but left in place to appear that way.

Félix was older than most of the kids in our barrio. He was around 15 then, with a thick head of hair, and squinty eyes. He didn't do well in school but he was very smart. Félix always looked for risky things to do, mostly because I think he got bored easily, and he just couldn't seem to sit still. The strongest kid of our group, (except for maybe Pupi who normally didn't hang around with us) Félix's muscles had started to bulge and he had a pimply, greasy face and the beginning of hair growing on his face and under his arms.

Whatever Félix said, we all listened to and followed, because he always was very macho and made us all feel like if we agreed with him that would make us macho too, or if we didn't, he might think that we maybe didn't think he was macho enough, and that wouldn't be good. This time, Félix dared me, Oscar, Jorge and Rique to go out with him into the bay, where the big ships came into the harbor. He said that he thought we could do it if he and the five of us took turns rowing and we had a sail to catch the wind just right.

Estás loco? Oscar said. Félix nodded and cracked a smile.

Félix figured if we could get to the river early in the morning before people began arriving at the market, then took the boat out into the mouth of the San Juan when the morning breezes blew from the hills above the city towards the bay, we could raise the sail and get over the rough water coming out of the river before anyone realized the boat had been taken.

I knew this was a bad idea, that it could be dangerous, and that if my father ever found out a bunch of us kids took a boat from a local *político* and went out into the bay without permission, he would probably not let me play in the streets for the rest of the summer vacation. I was also scared of the beating and humiliation I would probably get in front of all my friends and neighbors, but I tried to put that out of my mind.

The whole thing took careful planning. Félix's idea was to get a long *tendedera* pole (a hardwood pole traditionally used to raise a "*tendedera*" or clothesline in yards) that we could use as a mast on the rowboat. One night he went by the river and nailed four pieces of wood into the center of the boat towards the front, forming a rectangular slot into which the bottom of the mast could be wedged and from which it could be raised or lowered. To the top of the eight-foot *tendedera* pole he screwed an eyebolt, through which we could run a rope that tied at either end to a five-foot broomstick to which he had sewed the top of makeshift square sail of about the same width, and which rolled down and up, like the ships of the Vikings.

We made the rectangular sail out of two large white sugar cane sacks from papi's grocery and joined them with fishing line. Jorge painted a yellow sun in the center of the sail. The lower corners of the sail had ropes tied to each end which Félix said we could tie to the sides of the boat and would use later to control the direction and tension of the sail.

Félix had figured that with the five of us on the boat and a strong wind, the boat would be top-heavy once the sail was up. He found a heavy lead pipe, about the length of the boat. He threaded a rope through it, and tied each end at the front and to the back of the boat on the day of the trip. When we rowed out into open water, we lowered it off one side into the water to dangle parallel and so it in the water beneath the center length of the boat, about two feet in deep. Félix figured this us enough weight below the water to keep the boat from tilting when the sail was up. We did not question him, because he was smart and older, and because other than rowing, none of us knew anything about boats and we had never gone out on the bay.

The day of the trip came. Across from the Plaza del Mercado and just over the bridge and upriver on the Rio San Juan, there was a slaughter house. At the end of each day, the *carniceros* dumped wasted parts of animal carcasses, like hearts, legs, and intestines into the river. That morning, there must have been ten or twenty stray dogs, and several turkey vultures feasting on the remnants of the bloody piles by the river's edge.

The smell of rotting meat and intestines was so bad that when the wind changed direction across the river from the slaughterhouse, we had to tie handkerchiefs to cover our faces to keep from vomiting.

A little further down the river, was the place where big grey fish usually swirled in the current, especially around the columns of the San Juan Bridge. They attacked the floating intestines and other chunks of what was left of dead cows, and they were crazy-like, sometimes even biting each other. I learned in school that sharks could swim up the mouth of rivers, even in freshwater. All they needed was to smell blood. And blood there was...

We finally took Uncle Samuel's rowboat about 7:00 that morning from the dock off Calle Cuba into where the two rivers merged. The tide was going out. Jorge was kind of chubby and about the same height and build as Rique, so Félix told them to sit towards the back of the rowboat. Oscar and I sat up on the front and started rowing to the center of the river.

Félix kneeled near the middle of the boat, with his back to the bow, and held the base of the *tendedera* pole in the center slot, with the top end resting on Jorge's shoulder, and the broomstick with the sail folded, held by Rique. The lead pipe lay by Félix's hip, ready to be lowered over the port side and into the water as soon as he gave me and Rique the order.

We bobbed as the currents of the Rio San Juan neared the bay, causing some rough rocking just down from the San Juan Bridge. The water was murky, and I didn't see any fins breaking the surface by the time we reached the bridge. But the oily streaks leaked from bloody cow intestines as they floated by made me think I should start praying to the Virgen of La Caridad, patron Saint of Cuba to give me courage and put the shark thoughts out of my mind...just in case.

Santa María, Madre de Díos, ora por nosotros, I prayed and kneeled on the boat as I touched my forehead, then the middle of my chest, then left shoulder, and then right shoulder. I kissed the three fingers of my right hand.

We made it through the silty green waters where the river currents met the bay and then started to see streaks of aquamarine along the shallow sandy edges that marked the entrance into the bay. The water here began to clear but very quickly it became very deep and blue so we lost sight of the bottom.

Blue water, blue sky, and there's the bay! Jorge squealed.

The breeze began to pick up and Félix signaled for me and Oscar to pull up our oars and help lower the pipe over the side. Félix stood, cradled the sail pole and pulled it up straight, as Jorge and Rique positioned the sail and readied it for it to unfold. Félix tied the bottom of the mast to the base of the boat, handed me and Jorge two other ropes tied to the top of the mast. One I attached to the bow, and the other Jorge tied onto an eyehook on thc stern.

As Félix ordered Rique to unroll the sail, a gust of wind came from behind. The sail snapped and puffed up, tilting the bow down with a sudden jerking of the boat forward. The surprise jolt almost flipped Rique overboard. Within minutes we were slicing through the water and headed for the center of the bay, yellow sun insignia bulged, and the edges of our sail flapped as the wind changed direction. Rique worked a rudder Félix had built and attached to the rowboat, and Félix, our confident *Capitán*, shouted one command after the other. The boat now moved in a straight line.

Coñó, que fantástico! Rique screamed, howled, and threw his arms in the air. All I could think of was what we had done by ourselves and how free I felt. I thanked the Virgen de La Caridad and begged her to also make sure none of my dad's friends recognized me as we pulled away from the dock near La Plaza.

The next four hours went by in what seemed like minutes. Once we got out about what felt like a mile into the bay, we lowered the sail and drifted. We laid on our backs and looked up at the sky. Later, we ate saltine crackers and yellow cheese, and drank Coca Colas which I had snuck out of my father's grocery the night before. We threw the empty green bottles into the water and watched them spin as they sank, air bubbles rose as they blended with the color of the water and then disappeared to the bottom.

We bobbed in the waves and heard the seagulls overhead and the distant hum of traffic along El Prado, the major bayside road in the neighborhood of Versailles. Occasionally, puffs of breeze misted us with salty sea spray, which dried on our skin, leaving whitish salty crusts. Félix licked the salt off his muscled arms as he flexed them. God he was so macho it made us proud he was our *Capitán*...

I looked to the north shore of the bay where just a few months before, papi had taken me to the loading docks there to visit a friend of his who worked at the restaurant of the then Club de Oficiales (Navy Officer's Club). It was 1961 and I remembered seeing the largest cargo ship ever docked near the Officer's Club.

The name of the ship was in strange letters, which I think must have been Russian writing. The ship had a large red flag with a yellow Sickle and Hammer insignia. By 1961, many Russian ships came to Matanzas harbor. Huge cranes unloaded new mini-buses onto the dock. (Later I learned that these were made in Czechoslovakia and that they were imported to Cuba for public transport—which was a disaster, because the air-cooled engines on the buses overheated and died in the hot and humid Cuban climate.)

The Russian navy unloaded other cargo, including large wooden boxes the length of a Chevrolet, with what looked like machinery inside. (Later I learned that people who were in the know told my father that these were Russian missile parts.) After the ship was unloaded, Cuban *estivadores* loaded hundreds of sacks with sugar cane, rice, beans and fresh fruit onto the ship. I had heard that the Russians loved Cuban food. I remembered that many of the sailors had reddish hair, pale pink skin, and angled faces. They shouted at each other in gruff, snappy voices, like they were angry but they weren't really arguing, it was just the way they talked Russian.

The sea breeze felt great out in the middle of the bay. We laid on our backs, legs hung over the sides of the boat as we drifted in open water. Then it seemed like a cloud had suddenly blocked the sun, putting our little boat under a dark shadow. But there weren't any clouds. The water became choppy and we heard the loud clanging of what sounded like factory engines. As we sat up and turned in the direction of the eclipsing shadow, a piercing whistle rattled my chest.

Que está pasando? What is happening?

Jorge bolted up to a sitting position. A large tanker was but a hundred and fifty yards away and sailed in a slant pattern straight for us. The wake of the ship as it passed changed the horizon and suddenly, we bobbed like little rubber ducks in the shadow of the oncoming Russian giant. We thought that probably the sailors hadn't even seen us, or if they did, they probably either didn't care, or couldn't turn away from us in time. All I thought of was my father being mad at me if I fell overboard and drowned after stealing a boat. What would the Russians say?

We were soaked as waves from the wake of the ship poured into the rowboat. We grabbed onto the sides with one hand and bailed with tin cans we had brought along with the other. Félix then took over. The boat had about four inches of water in it. He leaned over, cut the rope holding the pipe with his penknife, flung the mast and sail overboard and grabbed both oars, shoving me and Oscar out of the way. He began to row furiously from the wake of the tanker as we bailed desperately in panic. This was it. We stole Samuel's boat and God and the Russians decided to punish us.

Rápido, boten agua! Quick, keep bailing, Félix screamed.

Two more loud toots from the ship's whistle, and the shadow began to move past us. Uncle Samuel's rowboat pitched and bobbed wildly, out in the middle of Matanzas Bay. We could smell the diesel fumes trail from the smokestacks of the ship. The Virgen of La Caridad would make sure those damned Russians would get what they deserved for nearly killing us that afternoon. We made it back to the dock on the San Juan, unnoticed by anyone as the boat thieves that we were, but we swore to never do this again.

The name Matanzas means "massacre" in Spanish, but it wasn't until about thirty years later when I was reading about how the city of my birth got its name, that I discovered Matanzas was given this name based on an account in the late 1600's in which a group of Spanish invaders crossed the bay towards an aboriginal camp near the mouth of the river. As the story goes, the soldiers approached some natives, and forced them to help them cross the bay. Not trusting the strange bearded men, while out in deeper water, the natives flipped the Spaniards' boats in revenge, and swam to safety. The Spaniards' heavy metal armor would not give them the luxury of floating, and most of the Spaniards drowned. I thought about us and the Russians.

18
PAPALOTE WARS

Parque René Fragas: "*Cradle of the great sport stars of Matanzas... inviting place of recreation for children, lovers and the elderly, this park stands as the watchful guardian of a lovely city.*" Cubatech Travel, 2020.

I used to love running up and down the staggered stone terraces, jumping off the walls onto the nearby lush grass and rolling down the hill. To us kids, this was just *el parque,* where we played all kinds of games with abandon. I especially liked looking towards the bay from one of the stone benches, *watching* eight or ten *papalotes* at any one time high above in the sky. They looked like multicolored paper eagles gliding gracefully in the breezes that blew over the hills towards the *Valle of Yumurí.*

El parque was an ideal place for kite-flying because below its terraces was an open grassy field the size of three- or four-square city blocks. There were no *postes eléctricos,* and no *cables* to tangle the kite lines.

In Matanzas, one didn't buy kites in a store. You either knew someone who handcrafted them for sale or as a hobby, or you made one yourself with whatever materials you could find at home. My first *chiringa* was a folded triangular piece of paper, with a harness of short pieces of string tied to a *pita,* or string line made of thin cotton, and a "tail" or *cola,* made of very thin ribbon from a remnant of a dress abuela was making. My *chiringa* was the rudimentary kite kids usually made on their first attempt at making kites. But try as I did, running down *Calle San Gabriel,* even on a breezy day, my best *chiringa* barely got 10 or 20 feet above the ground and not for more than 15 or 20 seconds of flight before it plummeted unceremoniously to a puddle on the street. Enter *Tío Yayo.* One day he brought me a handful of reeds he picked by the river. They would be the frame for my first real *papalote.* Abuela bought me sheets of *pañuelos de papel,* colored tissue paper from *El Polaco's* store across the street. We built my first *papalote,* definitely a step up from the many failed *chiringa* prototypes I had struggled to make.

Maiden flight: P*arque René Fragas.* Tío Yayo insisted on flying the kite. The long tail and the fragility of the beautiful *Buena noche,* as I named my *papalote,* along with my total inexperience of being nine years old, convinced me I had no business with the first flight. But I got to be first assistant.

I held the the *Buena Noche* by its frame, out in the middle of the open field, in a directíon where the breeze was coming towards me. The morning sun had come up strong, drying most of the dew off the grass, which kept the long tail of my kite from getting wet. Tío let out enough line as I held the kite taught above my head. I could smell the sweet frangipani wafting from the flowering bushes down the street as I stood there, in the breeze, waiting for his signal.

Uno, dos, y trés! shouted Tío. I released the kite and he ran, holding the string over his head into the oncoming breeze. The black comet peppered with yellow stars lifted, at first fluttering and zig-zagging, then with a gush, it began soaring upwards to at least one hundred feet above us. Tío let out almost all the line from the spool. There it was, my first real kite, flying way higher than I could have ever imagined, the long ribbon tail counterbalancing it, letting it glide in the breeze. A turkey vulture flew by, startling as it neared the flying black hexagon.

Over the next several weeks I would launch *The Buena Noche* several times, with the help of Vento, who lived on the street bordering the *parque*. That is, until one particularly windy day. My line snapped, and the kite flew away untethered, dropping down into some trees a couple of blocks away. Much to my disappointment, we were not able to retrieve the kite.

Some days later, I had built a new kite. I didn't give it a name. Bright red with yellow stars. I went over to the park. By then I had begun to learn hand movements, jiggling the line in certain ways, positíoning my arm such that I felt more comfortable maneuvering my kite to move right, left, and even dive and recover. *It was all in the wrist and the feel of the string,* like Tío said.

When I arrived at the park one Saturday morning, I was surprised to find thirty or forty people there. There were many kids older than me and some stood around the edges of the field, while smaller groups clustered about, scattered on the grassy expanse. There must have been 15 or 20 kites readying for flight on the ground, as well as six or seven that were already high and flying. I noticed the groups usually had one person with the kite, another that held it, plus one or two more who seemed preoccupied with tying things onto the tails. Some grown men without kites stood around by the street near

Vento's house in groups, talking excitedly among themselves as they pointed at the kites.

Are you ready, Vento? Hold it steady, make sure the tail isn't tangled. Uno, dos, trés...let go!

People started getting more kites up in the air, and I readied mine while Vento held it. After three tries we got it flying and I began letting out line steadily. The breeze was quite strong that day, and the sun shone brightly, but my red kite was easy to spot even with the glare. A perfect kite-flying day and a beautiful kite at that. I became a little anxious as my *papalote* was flying well, but it seemed like with so many kites in the air, it would be hard to avoid lines crisscrossing and mid-air collisions.

Oooh, mira mira, look up! pointed some kid to the sky towards a kite that had gotten loose as it blew away towards the terraces. People were clapping and cheering and I couldn't understand why at first. Then another, and it looked briefly as if a third kite had sidled close to it, dived down and the tail tugged the tangled line of the other kite, as the first kite snapped off, to be swept by the breezes. Kids were screaming and running after loose kites everywhere.

He cut it, look at it go! Let's go get it! yelled another from the center of the field, pointing with excitement towards a rather large *papalote* as it tumbled towards the ground. More cheering and clapping. Kids ran excitedly, clustering around the downed kite and scrambling, frenzied, even shoving each other, and fighting to get at the grounded kite.

I held my *papalote* taught, and felt the steady tug and vibratíons from the shifting air currents pulling on the line. I took my eyes briefly off the kite to look for other flyers around me, and suddenly, the tension on my line was gone! My heart sank as my red comet strayed, tail swinging wildly in erratic wide arcs. Some *hijo*-of-a-bitch had cut my line. I heard more cheering across the field, three kids from one of the clusters running in the directíon of my flyaway *papalote.* It was a sinking feeling when while walking off the field, spool in hand, I went past an older kid readying to fly and noticed the shiny, metallic strips attached crosswise on the tail of his kite. I had a closer look. Razor blades! I was so disgusted that I never even bothered to try and chase down my fly-away *papalote.* It was a shameful loss for me.

Papalote wars. That's what was going on. And I was so naïve thinking that everyone was there to watch the kites fly and enjoy the beauty of the colors in the sky. I then realized why there were so many older kids there, and I saw some of the grown men on the side exchanging *pesos* and laughing, cheering. People were betting! How could I have been so stupid!

I walked to Vento's house. His father was drinking a *cafecito* in the front yard watching the spectacle, and he told us all about the *papalote* wars on weekends. *There is only one rule: If you fly it and they cut it, it belongs to whoever catches it!* He said that the kids chasing the cut kites were "kite runners" who would sometimes run for many blocks, climb walls, even risk falling off roofs to retrieve a flyaway kite. People bet on who would cut a kite, even on who would be the first to capture it!

On my way home that day, I saw an older kid, maybe 13 or 14 looking up at a dangling kite on the power lines between two streetlamps. I did not recognize him as being from our barrio. He kept trying to jump up to reach for the remnant of line that dangled, hoping he could get to the tangled kite. Not succeeding, he began flinging rocks at the kite.

Hey, hey, why are you throwing rocks? I said. *You are just going to tear it up...*

He just kept flinging rocks.

Mi captura, mi papalote. It now belongs to me. If I can't have it, no one will!

I went home and sat in my room, totally demoralized and

furious. I decided I wouldn't be making or flying kites for a long while, and from then on if and when I did, I would make sure I went to the *el parque* on days and times where there were few people *empinando* their kites. And I would definitely be on the lookout for the *cuchillas* on tails.

In 2004, while at an airport, I picked up a paperback entitled *The Kite Runner*, a haunting tale about two childhood friends in Afghanistan. As I read through intriguing passages of kites flying, a deep nostalgia set in. The pages brought back intense memories of my *papalote* encounters of almost forty years earlier. I finished the book that same day and I couldn't get the thought of kites out of my mind.

I always thought the word, *papalote* was unusual. To my surprise, the word was not derived from Castilian Spanish. In fact, throughout Latin America and the Caribbean, different countries have at least 15 different words for kites, like *chiringa*, *barrilete*, *cometa*, and of course, *papalote*, which is what kites are commonly called in Mexico, Costa Rica, and Cuba. The word *papalote* comes from the *Náhuatl* tongue, one of the Uto-Aztec languages of Mexico, which was at one time spoken all over Mesoamerica.

Kite wars: The quest to seek out another's flying comet, cut it loose by whatever means, and then capture it for the spoils, even destroy it for the sake of conquest, control and perhaps a warped sense of ownership. A sport, perhaps for some, but no different in that sense for those who observe it or participate in it than that of the crowds and gladiators on the ground of an arena; perhaps more "civil" and less bloody, but nevertheless, misguided in its intentions, disrespectful of the beauty of color, and of the freedom of the flutter of a fragile object in flight.

How terribly ironic that *papalotl* is the noun for "butterfly" in Náhuatl.

The following week I purchased a commercial kite in the shape of a large blue and black butterfly. I flew my *papalotl* gracefully on the edge of the Gulf of Mexico on a breezy Pensacola Beach day and felt redeemed. I thought of *Parque René Fragas* and of my friend Vento, and I thought about what a lucky boy I had been to have sampled the wind currents and felt the transitory pull and tug of my red kite with the yellow stars as it glided and sailed high up above the hills of my *barrio* in Matanzas, nearly half a century ago. It was a feeling I could never convey to my daughters, now grown adults, nor to anyone who had never flown a kite, but one which I hoped I could share with my *nietos* one day. I looked up the plans for making a *papalote* from scratch, just like Tío Yayo taught me. I may need to find a different material than typewriter ribbon for the tail. Thankfully, razors will not be an issue. I have henceforth declared a permanent truce on *papalote* wars.

19
EGRESS

In mid-1961, two of my uncles who were in the United States petitioned the American Red Cross to assist my ailing mother, my asthmatic brother, my uncle, and my grandfather to leave Cuba accompanied by my father, my brother and me. My mother had an active thyroid condition, my uncle had a seizure disorder and my grandfather suffered from uncontrolled diabetes. Neither my uncle nor my grandfather nor my brother could get medication. My mother needed surgery to remove her thyroid gland.

The process for leaving Cuba was bureaucratic and emotionally burdensome. After we filed all the papers, we had to wait until we got clearance, and that notification came in a last-minute telegram from the Cuban Government not more than 48 hours before our scheduled exit. That telegram informed us we had permission to leave the country. This element of surprise I later found out was deliberately set up to assure that when people left the country, they would not have time to sell or give their belongings to friends and family, for the rules were that a condition for anyone leaving the country was to relinquish all their finances, real-estate and personal belongings for the benefit of *La Revolucíon.*

October 22, 1962. I was twelve years old. Abuelo was in bed, not feeling well that day. There was a knock at the door and abuela told me to answer it. It was the same man from the Housing Authority who came two days before. He brought the same notebook where two days earlier he had written down in detail every piece of furniture, every vase and figurine on every shelf, and any framed pictures on the wall of abuela's house. He had done the same at our house. On this day he double-checked every item he had recorded before to make sure it was still there.

The man had a very official way about him, and was not very pleasant. He acted like he was important. Abuela just followed behind him silently and gestured me to stay behind and to stay quiet. After double-checking his list of our belongings, he wrote out an official-looking slip, and handed it to my grandmother. She glanced at it, then placed it on the little table in the living room. I looked at it.

Aprobado. It had abuelo's name and address, and the date. The man signed his name, then took the keys to the house.

Remember, when you leave, just close la puerta behind you and make sure all the windows are closed. He put his notebook under his arm and left. That afternoon abuela told me it was time to take Yuti the dog to the butcher's house. I said nothing.

Ricardito do not worry, el carnicero will look after Yuti until we get back.

My father had been a close friend of the butcher and my family knew his family for many years. Abuela said I should be glad we were leaving Yuti with the butcher's family because with all the food shortages during *la Revolución,* Yuti would always have meat scraps to eat and bones to play with and she knew he wouldn't starve. That is what abuela said. I think she was trying to make me feel better. I had taken care of Yuti since he was a puppy. He belonged to Tío Yayo but he was really my dog.

Abuela closed the door behind her that afternoon and helped abuelo into the taxi. At 81, he was so sick with his diabetes that it was left to abuela and my uncle to take over all the work around the house and for the trip. We were scheduled on the first morning flight out of Rancho Boyero Airport in Habana to Miami. None of us in my family had ever been on an airplane.

On the morning of our flight my mother's cousin drove us to the airport. It was still dark. At 6:00 a.m. *milicianos* and police and military trucks and jeeps were everywhere. Two approached the car and waited for us to get out and drag our suitcases to the curb. Then as my father helped my abuelo hobble onto the sidewalk, one bearded *miliciano* soldier approached. His machine gun hung from a strap over his shoulder. I had never been that close to a machine gun. He leaned over to my father and said,

All flights to Miami are cancelled. Presidente Kennedy put a blockade around Cuba. Then with a sneer and a chuckle he looked at my grandfather, and said *Sorry, viejo, the Yankis will neither let you fly nor swim nor walk out of Cuba today. Why don't you just grab your maleta and go crawling back to where you came from? Viva la Revolucíon!*

We stayed in Cuba for another six months until we were given permission to fly to Mexico City.

20
LIMBO

Limbo: "Latin, *limbus*: noun. Referring to an "edge" or boundary; an uncertain period of awaiting a decision or resolution; a state of neglect or oblivion; in *Dante's Inferno*, Canto IV, the first circle of Hell where souls are not sinful, but lack the proper faith to gain entry to Paradise."

Before our slated egress on October 22, 1962, as required, we had surrendered our ration cards, papi had turned over his grocery store, and our house, our bank account, everything we owned. Abuelo and abuela had turned in their home to the *autoridades municipales* as well. Tío Yayo's car would become property of the state.

October 24, we are back in Matanzas. Our egress failed. My mother and father were silent, as if in deep mourning. Our flight to Miami had been blockaded by President Kennedy. Now what? This was not a plan under our control, and one outcome we could have never anticipated. Now we found ourselves with no home to go back to. What would we do?

A neighbor and former customer of my father happened to see us standing on the street, suitcases at our feet, at the doorstep of what 48 hours before had been our house on Calle Medio, but was now officially to become the property of the *26th of July Movement of the Revolution— the People's Revolution.*

That man, neighbor, friend, and customer of my father for many years and whom I shall refer to as Mr. "O", pulled papi aside. They spoke briefly, and although I strained to listen, I was unable to hear what they spoke about. My father appeared harried, told us he had to go somewhere, and he and "Mr. O" left in a hurry.

Mami knocked on Marta's door. Marta, a teacher, was a former classmate and lifelong friend of mami. When Marta opened the door and saw us standing there, absent my father, she threw her arms around mami, trembling,

Lydia, but...where is Pepe? Did they... was he arrested?

Marta rushed us into her house and helped sequester our suitcases inside. Mami detailed our entire ordeal. In the meantime, mami told me my father had gone to the *municipio* with our neighbor. He returned two hours later, drenched in sweat and looking haggard.

Que pasó, Pepe? Asked my mother, nervously.

Papi stood there for a moment, looked at my mother, and reached into his pocket. He took out two sets of keys and handed them to her. Mami instantly recognized them as the keys to our house and to abuela and abuelo's house. Both had strings tied with official looking little cardboard tags with our names and addresses.

I can explain later. It is complicado.

Marta fed us lunch, and we went back across the street to 23 ½ *Calle Medio.* Our house was as we had left it two days earlier. The lights worked, so the electricity had not been turned off. My grandparents and my uncle stayed at our house for most of the day and sat around or lay in bed, dazed and silent. My brother and I were bored, so we rummaged through our closet. He played with his trucks. I sat in the *terraza* out back, going through my old comic books as if nothing carthshat tering had happened, and in perhaps a distorted sense, I almost welcomed being back in our house.

Few words were spoken by the adults. As it became dark, papi walked abuela and Tío helped abuelo go to their house through a gate in the wall shared between our back yard and abuelo's side yard. Their electricity was also on. Papi walked back through the yard in the dark. We went to sleep without anything to eat that night.

The next morning, papi gathered us at the kitchen table. He told us that we had been given our house back, but that he couldn't get the *bodega* or his bank account, and that we wouldn't have the ratíon cards. He said that for the next few weeks we would have to stay at home, and that he would try to find food for us, now that he wouldn't be going back to work. We were kept from school and we were not to open the door to anyone or go outside to play. That was all papi said. I was furious.

But when can I go and get Yuti?

We would not be getting *Yuti* back. Papi said we might still get permission to leave the country if the *bloqueo* around Cuba was lifted, so we would just have to wait and be prepared to leave on short notice.

It would be better to let Yuti stay where he is. That would be the end of that conversatíon.

In anticipation that we might be leaving the country, for months before we received permission to leave for Miami, Tío and abuelo gradually began to give away or sell the fighting cocks, chickens, mallards, pheasants, and rabbits. Tío gave his monkey to a friend and freed most of his birds. We released the tropical fish back into the springs where we used to net them.

Yuti was left in the care of the butcher's family. Abuelo's house was now eerily quiet without the squawks and bird songs and screeches we had been used to for so many years. Abuela's garden was thriving.

Word must have gotten around to our neighbors about our misfortunes with the blockade and having to come back to Matanzas. I imagine many of them were hesitant to reach out, for fear that somehow the authorities might suspect they were sympathizing with or aiding *gusanos.* But an odd thing happened one day. There was a knock at abuela's door. By the time she looked through the peephole, whoever knocked was gone.

Abuela opened the door and found at the doorstep a familiar-looking large, rectangular tin can with a handle. The top of the can was covered with crumpled newspapers. The first time this happened abuela assumed it was a neighbor, as it was common in our *barrio* for people to go around with recycled olive oil cans to request *comida de cochinos* (pig slop) from their neighbors. Abuela lifted the can from her doorstep. After removing the newspapers, she found two very ripe mangos and a large avocado inside. Beneath the fruit was a pot covered with wax paper, filled with cooked white rice, black beans, and raw onions. She took out the food, put the crumpled newspaper back in the can, and placed it outside her doorstep. We never knew who was bringing us food, but every evening, there would be the can-at her doorstep.

There a few other things I clearly remember about the hundred and eighty-six days that followed: 1) Mami cried every day; she lost much weight and her eyes were bulging. 2) We didn't have to go to school. 3) We weren't allowed to listen to the Phillips radio or watch television. 4) Only Marta, mami's friend, and Toto, our across the street neighbors and his family were allowed to come to our house. 5) We were not to go outside of the house for any reason. 6) Having given or thrown away most of our personal belongings, we wore the same two changes of clothes from our luggage every other day. 7) Abuelo kept losing weight and he couldn't walk very well, even with his cane. He became forgetful and was very thirsty all the time. 8) Tío had dug up a large clay pot from abuela's back yard. He had buried it before we were to have left for Miami, thinking that we might be coming back to Cuba in a few months. Unbeknownst to us, Tío had collected American silver dollars for years. Eccentric as he was, he buried those in the pot, in tight rolls of paper he had immersed in car grease to prevent the coins from tarnishing. 9) Yuca, boniato, onions, became our every day staple. 10) Plucking juicy fruit from our plum tree and "relieving" the branches of abuelo's neighbors' tree from the weighty Filipino mangoes became my joyous weekly routine. 11) Abuela made soups with chunks of things I could never recognize, but they always tasted good. 12) *Tilo* tea from abuela's garden replaced the coffee we didn't have and the *yuca* grew like weeds.

Feeling trapped and thoroughly bored, I ended up memorizing all the words in my cartoon booklets. I taught myself to draw by copying some of the characters in my comic books. My Uncle Carlos had brought me some American comics from one of his yearly trips to the U.S. a couple of years before. I couldn't read the English captions, so I began tracing the characters with pencil onto tissue paper. Eventually I became good enough to draw them freehand. Batman was my first. My brother and I began playing together more. We had no friends that could come to our house and we were not allowed to go outside. I came to realize that not all prisons need have bars.

As I sat around day after day, bored and feeling sorry for myself, I didn't bother to understand then how bad it must have been for my parents and for the other adults in the family to cope with the uncertainty of our day-to-day situation. Papi managed to go to the municipal building once a month, where he paid electric bills with Tío's grease-stained, coin-collector grade American silver dollars. He minimized his outings, since everyone in our neighborhood knew him well, and he wanted to limit interactions that could potentially compromise our already precarious situation or put others at risk for any suspicion. Abuela began to leave silver dollars inside the can by her doorstep. Whoever of our neighbors or friends was bringing us food gave us from what they didn't have, and the economic situation in Cuba had become very difficult, so abuela felt it was only fair to provide some money in return for the kindness extended us, and for the expenses incurred.

Other "specifics" of those hundred and eighty-six days must be buried deeply in my psyche. Try as I may, I don't know how we were never arrested or how the neighborhood *Comité de Defensa* didn't come around to snoop, or how we got our house back and why the grocery was not returned to papi and Tío Yayo never would see his *Cheby* again. I cannot recall how and when we got word that we would leave Cuba again, but did remember a different man did show up to do inventory at both our houses before our second exit attempt. I have no recollection how we got to the airport the second time.

Years later, I was assigned the *Divine Comedy* for one of my college classes. As I read about "limbo," it was like suddenly, the hundred and eighty-six days in 1962-63 came back, flooding me with all sorts of uncomfortable memories. They were the days we lived in neglect, in oblivion, in a state of restraint and confinement, in a place of uncertainty. That was our limbo. I began to wonder about Dante's definition from Canto IV, "a sad place, lacking the violence of other levels of Hell..." and imagined whether it was people like us he wrote about prophetically, "the sinful, lacking in the proper faith to get into Paradise..." We had been in limbo. Then came the agony of leaving it all, and all over again. Yuti. Mango trees. Abuela's roses. Marching band. Comic books. Juanito. Cheby. Bueyvaca.

Many years later, during a reminiscing moment with my father about Cuba, we talked about finances. My father had grown up poor, and struggled for years to make his *bodega* business thrive. Having grown up during the Great Depression in the thirties in Cuba during Machado's presidency, he recalled that some people though hungry, went without at times, because of their pride. That is why papi kept a notebook by his cash register. He called it the "*fiado*" book. In it, he kept track of people who had bought groceries from him but could not pay him at the time of the sale. *Fiar* in Spanish means "to trust." Most people in papi's book paid their debts, and he would cross their names off accordingly.

There were a handful, he said, whose name remained on that book *for years. For those who couldn't pay, writing their name in the "trusted" book it made them feel like it wasn't a handout.*

But papi, some of these people owed you a lot of money. Why didn't you bother to collect it? Why didn't you tell them you wouldn't sell them any more groceries unless they paid what they owed you?

Papi chuckled. He told me that he knew these people well. They weren't just customers. They were trusted neighbors and friends. Many had families. Some were good people, others, maybe not-so-good-people, but nevertheless, people who had fallen on tough times and never seemed to get out from under the hardness of life. He told me he never really expected them to pay, but he always hoped that they would. It was the right thing to do, *To hope.*

Our conversation about the "*fiado*" book then took an

unexpected turn. Prior to and during the *Revolución de El Pueblo,* one of our neighbors had become a prominent activist for the *movimiento.* He was appointed to a position in the newly reformed Matanzas government, as a head of housing and urban affairs of sorts. Having just been on the job for over two weeks, he happened on my father one day on the street. It was October 24th to be exact, in front of our house. They spoke, then they went to the man's office at the *municipio.* Papi confided in him, and explained our horrendous situation in great detail. The man sat at his desk, reached into a drawer, and sorted through a set of keys. He looked at my father, reached over his desk and said,

Pepe, aquí tienes las llaves. (here are your keys). *No más conversacíon.*

Papi had left Mr. "O"'s office that day, trembling and speechless, but greatly relieved. The paperwork for surrendering our homes had not been officially processed. Mr. "O" risked his life and political reputation in doing what he did for us. My father knew the implications of his action. But he took the keys.

Ricar, just so you know, Mr. "O" had many entries my "Fiado" book, many going back several years, even before you were born. I only wish I hadn't destroyed the book before I had the chance to cross his name off. Life sometimes brings us great gifts when we least expect them...

Indeed. I don't believe my father ever told mami about Mr. "O" and what he had done for us. I wonder what ever happened to him.

21
THE SEVENTH ANGEL

When I stepped through the lobby of the Hotel Marlowe, and saw the half-inch wide cracks and uneven edges of the sidewalk, I knew that the trembling bed and rattling lamps in room 223 the night before was no bad dream: I had been in an earthquake.

It was April 29, 1963. The day marked my first morning in Mexico City. My first day of freedom as a Cuban refugee had begun as a truly earthshaking event. The evening before, I, along with my parents, my younger brother, my grandparents, and uncle had arrived on a bumpy flight from Habana. Besides the clothes we wore, we carried canvas suitcases containing no more than the allotted two changes of clothing for each traveling passenger. The militia at the Habana airport had strip-searched us prior to boarding the Aeromexico flight. I remembered how they glared at abuelo and thought it was funny he wore suspenders and a belt. Mr. Castro's rules were simple: "expatriates-to-be" were allowed no money, no jewelry, and no personal belongings upon leaving the country. Any such items were considered luxuries, would be confiscated by the soldiers, and might have given them reason to threaten to hold a passenger, even a thirteen-year-old boy like me, from leaving the country. The soldiers didn't know about the capsule I had swallowed earlier that morning.

It was a beautiful first Saturday morning in Mexico City. My parents tried to make small talk, being matter-of-fact and upbeat, as they stood in the lobby, treading air. I waited for my father to direct our first activity in this unknown city, on this most unusual day. I pictured myself and my family as not unlike a bevy of quail raised in captivity, now suddenly released into an open field to fend for ourselves. We had not eaten anything since the dinner served on the plane the day before. At thirteen, I was mature enough to recognize when my parents tried to act calm when in fact they were scared and upset, not knowing what to do next. The truth was we had no money to eat. We had no money, period. My uncles in New Jersey had pre-paid the first two nights at the Marlowe and were to have cabled a money order to the hotel, but it was Saturday, and according to the manager, the money had not arrived. My brother, René was barely seven years old, and he tugged incessantly at my mother's skirt, begging for breakfast. My father stood there, hands hung idly at his sides. It was like the reality of the moment paralyzed him.

Señor... came a soft voice from across the lobby. *I know where yew can haf' some bery nice coffee and tortillas for yewr whole family...Please come with me,* motioned the bellhop, hands pointed towards the street. My little brother shrieked, and urged everyone to follow the little man who wore the ill-fitting uniform, out of the lobby and down the street. My father's face blanched with embarrassment as we turned the corner and were escorted into a narrow alleyway through double doors above which hung a peeling, hand-painted sign which read, "Cantina de Angelita." I remembered the large red clay pot outside the entrance, and the multicolored flowers that hung from it. A nutty aroma of fresh corn tortillas wafted from inside the door.

Before my father could speak, "Victor," as the bellhop introduced himself, interjected, *You dun't haf 'to pay for thee food today if you weesh, Señor... I can make it so you can pay Angelita at thee end of thee week for the whole week of breakfast.*" My father exhaled, cold drops of sweat coursed down his temples. With an approving nod, we sat down to perhaps one of the most welcomed meals my family ever had. Hungry as I had been, my mother reminded me about the capsule and how I was to only have liquids till it "passed" ... I watched my family eat tamales and egg omelets and I resigned myself to sip on sweet lemonade.

Victor was an odd-shaped little man who looked like he was in his fifties, but was probably fifteen years younger. He had a large head with thinning jet-black hair which he combed back from his forehead, and which always looked wet. His head smelled of cheap brilliantine. He had a kind, self-effacing smile, which he shyly displayed in between soft sentences. Victor walked with a peculiar waddle, exaggerated in its oddity by a slight hunchback posture. His ample-fitting navy bellhop uniform was clearly not tailored for him. The pants' legs were sewn with light colored thread which surfaced in skips around the dark cloth. His shirt, though white, looked slept-in, and the shirt cuffs which extended about three inches below the sleeves of his epauletted jacket, were frayed on the edges. He wore a ribbon-thin bowtie which hung unevenly from a rumpled collar.

Victor had never met us until that morning, but introduced the family to Angelita like we were his long-lost first-degree relatives, exalting the fact we had just arrived from Cuba and didn't know the city. He assured us that Angelita would welcome us to Mexico City and show us the neighborhood. Angelita was a woman in her late seventies with olive skin, ample arms, and a lovely smile. She, despite being dressed humbly, exuded the simple elegance of a woman who had probably turned many heads in her youth. A gold crucifix hung around her neck. My father explained that Cuban food was traditionally not spicy. Angelita accommodated us by agreeing to prepare meals according to our preference, and without chilies. My father delegated abuela to share recipes. Angelita made breakfast and a daily mid-late afternoon meal for an agreed-upon price, and we paid her on a weekly basis. Victor's face-saving maneuver reprieved my father from conjecturing payment by the end of the week.

Two days passed, and the money from my uncles in New Jersey had not arrived. We could not afford a long-distance telephone call. The hotel manager was not sympathetic. My father became frantic. All he could think about was the money we would owe Angelita in just a few days...plus the hotel bill. As a grocer in Cuba my father had been an honorable man. He never borrowed and he always believed in keeping his word. My father fumbled nervously with the empty wallet he had rescued from exile, somehow thinking that if he opened and closed it repeatedly, money would materialize. There would be no sleep for him that night.

All our hopes were now dependent on the capsule. My uncle, who had originally conceived the idea of fashioning a rubber capsule by joining the cut tips of two baby nipples, placing them one into the other, and heat-sealing them with rubber glue had experimented with similar "prototypes." At first, feeding the date-size capsules soaked in mineral oil to Yuti on several occasions provided a challenge. As long as the dog was allowed only liquids, the capsules seemed to "pass" uneventfully. I was elected by default to "carry the package" as they referred to it during public conversation. Castro's men would never suspect a thirteen-year-old boy of smuggling American dollars out of Cuba. Besides, my mother and father explained that my uncle, an epileptic, might vomit if he had a seizure, thus giving them away, that abuelo was a brittle diabetic and too feeble to swallow, and that she and my father were both too anxious and might give themselves away. My grandmother, I knew, was too proper a lady to suffer the indignity of the task.

It was the only time my parents ever asked me to lie. If for some reason I was to have been caught, I was to tell the authorities that I found the money, was afraid to tell my parents about it, so I swallowed it. I had rehearsed and practiced the routine many times, by swallowing grapes soaked in mineral oil. I recalled the nauseating taste of the oil and the tactile sensation, the choking feel of the grape as it descended through my mid-chest and eventually into my stomach. I knew that in agreeing to use me as a "mule" my parents must have been desperate. When desperate, I learned, people did desperate things. At the time this was a challenging adventure to a thirteen-year-old who didn't know better. I never realized until many years later how precarious an act this would be, both physiologically and politically speaking.

The following day, just past midnight the capsule finally exited my gut. *Papi, look!!* I shouted from the toilet, awakening the whole family. The two tightly-rolled, American hundred-dollar bills inside it were extracted, dry and completely intact, much to everyone's great relief.

Over the next several weeks in Mexico City, we settled into a routine: Angelita showed us where the open-air market and the cathedral were. My grandmother visited the church every day. She said prayer had no side effects, and it didn't cost money to pray. Victor entertained me during his shifts at the hotel by allowing me to shuttle bags of arriving guests into the elevator while my parents spent time shopping for bargain fruit and days-old bread, which became our late evening "filler" meal. Victor always made it a point to allow me to share his tips, which made me feel that much more important. I prided myself in giving what little money I "earned" to my father, which I knew would guarantee Papi's approval to let me continue to "work" with Victor.

The Marlowe was a "one star," rent-by-the-week hotel on a side street just one block off the famous Alameda drive in the heart of Mexico City. It was frequented by budget travelers, itinerant ballerinas who danced with the Ballet Folklórico, and by "The Koreans," as Victor called them. This was a group of four Asian men who came to Mexico City and stayed at the Marlowe often. Victor thought they owned racehorses, and he could tell when they won big, because the Koreans would pull up to the hotel lobby in limousines and he would help them load cooking utensils, exotic vegetables and garlicky-smelling meats and liquor bottles on the elevators. During these "victory parties," the Koreans were usually flanked by high-heeled, beautiful Mexican *palomas* bejeweled and smothered in cheap perfume and tacky facial rouge. They partied at the penthouse way into the late hours. Victor had said that although the Koreans and their ladies were probably not living as "good Catholics," they always treated Victor well, and so he treated these men and their escorts likewise, with respect.

In the following weeks, I became Victor's unofficial apprentice. The hotel manager didn't seem to mind, recognizing the difficult situation my family faced, not being allowed to enter the United States until our immigration papers cleared. In Mexico, it was not unusual for children to work at an early age, so a thirteen-year-old bellhop's assistant would not have seemed out of place. For me, the opportunity was a blessing. It was a way to pass the time, and any time I earned a few pesos from carrying luggage, I felt like I contributed to my family. Besides, at thirteen, and weathering the surges of pre-pubescent hormonal storms, I was thrilled to escort the shapely ballerinas who stayed at the hotel to-and-from the elevator into their rooms. I loved the smell of perfume when I entered their rooms. I would at times visit them while they sunbathed on the roof under the pretense of asking if they wanted refreshments from the restaurant. I marveled at their slender, pearly thighs. I think the ladies perceived me as cute because I paid so much attention to them, constantly asking if they needed anything to let me know. All along I just figured that this was just not friendliness on their part, but that they were all in fact, secretly and irresistibly in love with me.

Our family had to stay in Mexico City for the next several months. I noticed that my mother's face became gaunt. She had always been a pretty woman, but now it seemed as if her beauty was consumed by worry. Papi's clothes hung loosely. I knew they purposely went with little food so that my grandparents, my brother and I, along with my frail uncle would have enough to eat from week to week. I developed a Mexican Spanish accent, and learned many idioms and curse words from playmates in the park. Victor often told me stories about his wife and his two children, and how he would arrange sometime for our families to meet and visit. It was always odd to me that after shifts ended, Victor almost miraculously vanished from the hotel, and when seen leaving, always appeared in a hurry to be somewhere. Victor was usually vague about his whereabouts, and told me it was because he worked two jobs. Victor had said he lived near the plaza but never volunteered a street address.

On Sundays, even when he was not on duty, Victor brought bags of fruit or rolls of freshly baked bread which he left with the concièrge, and which he expressly noted were for "the Cubans." It was difficult to know how Victor managed this, and when I or my father saw him during the week, we thanked him profusely, Victor always acknowledged that it was no trouble and it was his pleasure. Victor always maintained that he and his family had more food than they needed and that if they didn't use it, the fruit would spoil and the bread would get stale. The three months my family spent in Mexico City were beyond idle. I was stalked and nearly kidnapped by a child molester at Alameda Park, had it not been for my newly made friends who intervened. A shop owner of a leather goods store directly across from our hotel was found brutally murdered and neither the killer nor a motive was ever found. Papi and mami had befriended the victim and his wife two weeks earlier and were questioned by the police on more than one occasion. Our family's entry into the United States was delayed by my father having had an abnormality suspicious for tuberculosis on his chest x ray and by the interminable iterations of Mexican bureaucracy. My uncles in the United States wrote that their funds to cover our living expenses were rapidly depleting. Papi's wallet was stolen by a pickpocket on a crowded city bus in broad daylight. My seven-year-old brother's asthma was flaring and we had neither medications nor the funds to buy medicine. But we had Victor, and Angelita. We had my grandmother's prayers to Our Lady, the Virgin of Guadalupe. Victor had the Koreans. I had ballerinas falling in love with me on a daily basis. I learned to play soccer on the same soil where Aztec warriors battled centuries earlier to protect their major temple, just blocks off the Alameda Park.

On a Friday morning in June, our family received notice from the American Consulate that our entry to the United States had been approved. My uncles sent funds to cover the cost of the flight. We were to fly from Mexico City to La Guardia Airport in New York the following Sunday.

We said our good-byes to Angelita and to Victor that week. My grandmother visited the cathedral one last time, and gave thanks to the saints and to God for our freedom. She told God in her prayers that she appreciated that God never gave anyone in life more than they could handle, but that she perhaps wished He had not had so much confidence in her! Victor apologized for never having had a chance to have us over to meet his family and visit his home. We had no words to express the kindness Victor and Angelita had shown us for the past three months. My father took his black dress belt and his coin purse and had my mother wrap them in colored paper, with a ribbon and a note of thanks. I gave them as a gift to Victor. My mother brought carnations for Angelita.

I remembered being wedged into the back seat of the taxi van that Sunday morning on our way to the airport. We were all silent, glad to be finally joining the rest of our family in the United States, yet sad to be leaving the people that gave us a home when we lacked one, and the beautiful souls whose path we crossed during our tribulations in a foreign city. The van had traveled about three blocks from the hotel. We stopped at a traffic light. From the window of the taxi, I glanced towards a nearly empty parking lot on the far corner of the intersection, typical of the many such facilities throughout the city, which were often staffed by live-in attendants.

I had walked past this parking lot many times, but had never noticed that built against the back wall of a tall building was a shabbily-constructed wood and cardboard shack whose roof was made of rusted corrugated metal sheets anchored by bricks. A small charcoal stove was outside the door, and I made out the backside of a woman leaning over it, cooking tortillas. She held an infant in a shawl wrapped around her hip. Outside the door of the shack was a man in a rumpled white shirt and dark jacket. He was cutting the hair of a young boy who sat shirtless on a wooden crate. The man looked like was in his fifties, but was probably fifteen years younger. He had a large head with thinning jet-black hair combed back from his forehead. He stood with a peculiar posture, exaggerated in its oddity by a slight hunchback. His ample-fitting bellhop uniform was clearly not tailored for him.

22
ADJUSTING

First Day

Although Horace Mann Elementary School No.9 was an architecturally attractive Beaux-Arts style building built in the 1930's, the brick and cornices were stained by years of soot and the drab-looking facade gave the school a dreary, institutional look. The schools I went to in Cuba were one story, spread out, with palm trees, flowers and gardens around courtyards and trellises with flowers in the entry. The windows were always open to let in the breeze.

Scaling the three-leveled set of steps and going through the heavy dark metal doors to the Office that first morning in School No.9 as I trailed my cousin Carlos and Aunt Mery terrified me. The polished granite floors, the smell of commercial disinfectant and the sterile look of the place alone was daunting. Aunt Mery gave the person in the office an envelope with papers signed by my parents, which I presume were my enrollment materials, as my parents didn't speak English and didn't accompany me to school that day. I know they were my papers because I recognized my powder-blue Cuban passport. The woman at the office wore dark rimmed glasses. Her bleached blond hair was strange, like nothing I had ever seen. Instead of normal hair, it looked like a lacquered beehive attached to her head, and it wobbled ever so slightly as one single unit when she nodded. Mery and the woman spoke in rapid English I could not understand, and after stamping and stapling some documents, she returned my passport, handed my aunt a sheet, and pointed her down the hallway and up the stairway.

I prayed that Carlos and I would be in the same class, but God, no, Aunt Mery walked me into a classroom on the third floor and said something to the eighth-grade teacher as she left me.

Hasta luego, Ricar, todo está bien. Buena suerte. All is good. So long. Good luck!

There I stood, and the teacher closed the door as Aunt Mery walked away with my cousin down the hall. I felt like a mouse left in a box, with about thirty hungry house cats and a larger cat just eyeing me. Mr. Minogue, the teacher, was an older, heavy-set man with a large head and curly greying-blond hair and bushy-wild, eyebrows. His blue pin-striped suit reeked of cigarette smoke, and reminded me of the way Tío Yayo's suit smelled. Mr. Minogue gazed at the piece of paper my aunt had handed him, furled one eyebrow, and cleared his throat. In a deep baritone voice he said,

Buenes deeahs, Richardo. Can you habla English? The large cat growled, and all other cat eyes were on me.

All I could manage was a blank stare and a cold sweat. Mr. Minogue pointed me to an empty seat in the back and handed me a thick book, *History of the United States.* I sat, holding the book tightly, because it was the only thing I could do to keep my hands from trembling. Class had obviously started before I arrived, and no introductions were made, which was fine by me because I had an intense desire to just evaporate. Mr. Minogue then wrote "*page* 358" on the blackboard and clapped as he shook the chalk dust from his hands. He looked up. *Let's begin.*

I quickly intuited that the first 357 pages of the history book had probably been covered the year before during seventh grade. I could not understand anything Mr. Minogue said. Later on, we had mathematics class. I was totally confused. Division was done completely differently than I had learned in Cuba. The divisor was where the dividend was in Cuban mathematics, and the quotient and remainder were likewise displaced from the way I had been taught. Fractíons were also added and subtracted in a very strange way. No way I should learn United States History from the last half of the period since the country began as a country and worse yet, I wasn't willing to not know what to do with my divisor and dividend! Although I had finished seventh grade in Cuba, I knew I didn't belong in the American eighth grade. That night I explained my frustration to Aunt Mery and after talking with my parents and much begging, she took me to school the next day and requested I be moved to seventh grade. Starting the history book from the beginning would be a good thing, I thought.

Mister Sherry, Seventh grade

Mister. Cherry, that is what I heard his name was, not "Mr. Sherry," which was the way he pronounced and spelled it. He was probably in his late twenties or early thirties, with a kind face and a bland smile. Mr. Sherry walked me to a center aisle, towards the back third of the class, and pointed me towards the only empty seat in the classroom. I felt like I was running a gauntlet walking up the aisle with multiple sets of eyes tracking me. But I kept my gaze towards my shoes as I walked. The desk looked just like my school desk in Cuba, with a slot for storing books underneath. Kids in New Jersey scratched and carved names on the desktop, just like we did in Cuba, which made me feel better.

Senk' jew, Mister Cherry. I sat down and crossed my hands over the desktop.

A girl seated to my right on the other aisle looked at me, chuckled sheepishly, almost as if she knew just how I felt. That would be Mrynn. And I would soon find out she *did* know just how I felt, as she had just arrived from Poland as an immigrant to New Jersey and was new to School No. 9, and *Mister Cherry's* seventh grade class, just as I was. Myrnn and I would soon learn about the suffering of being strangers.

That morning, class was interrupted when a loud bell began ringing throughout the building. The sound echoed off the granite floor in the hallways. Everyone became excited. Mr. Sherry said something to the class, and everyone then crawled under the desks and crouched, hands covering both ears, head tucked down, facing the floor. Everyone except for me and Mrynn. Mr. Sherry demonstrated and we followed suit. We all stayed in this posítion until the bell stopped, then Mr. Sherry gave the directions for people to get back to their seats. We never did this in school in Cuba. I am sure they didn't do this in Poland, either. What craziness was this?

The following week a siren went off in the mid-morning. Mr. Sherry began giving directions in English, guiding students to line up and leave the classroom in orderly file. We lined up in the hallway, then went down three flights of steps, alarm still ringing, out to the courtyard, where all the various classes were doing the same. We lined up outside in a cold September breeze for about a half hour, then went back in the building when the sound stopped, and resumed class as if nothing had happened. What kind of craziness was this? Was this how the kids got their exercise in America? *Los locos.*

That night I asked my cousin Carlos about the loud bell and crouching under the desks the week before and also about the siren and lining up downstairs in the courtyard at the school No. 9 and what this meant.

You go under the desk and cover yourself in case there is an atomic bomb coming. That is so you can protect your major organs. This seemed so bizarre that I thought I either did not understand him or that he was playing with me.

The siren is in case there is fire, it is to practice how to get out of a fire in the building. It is called a "Fire Drill," you know, what-do-you-call-it in Spanish, yes, a "Práctica en caso de incendio..." that's it. "Compréndes?"

But the windows in the school No. 9 could not be opened from the inside...What if there was a real fire? It took us almost a half hour to line up and walk down three flights of steps to the outside. If there was a fire, we could have been barbecued inside in the half hour it took us to leave the building! I guess they didn't want any kids jumping out the window if there was fire in school No. 9. *Los locos.*

Homework

My Uncle Miguel had given me a paperback English/Spanish dictionary to use. Even still, I felt totally lost during class in the day, barely catching a word here and there. I could tell Mrynn was lost too, but we couldn't commiserate with each other about our quandary other than by sign language and facial expressions. At night I would try to do my homework: I would translate word for word what was in the text book to Spanish, write it down and try to follow directions as best I could, then try to translate what I thought were the answers to English. It was agonizing. My cousin Carlos was one year behind me but he was fluent in English. He wasn't much help, however, because he was busy with his own homework and it was effortful for him to explain things. So, I had to gut things out. I felt remiss that for two nights in a row I knew I had Geography homework to do but was unable to complete it.

Richardo, I need to speak with you after class... Mr. Sherry was never threatening, in fact he had a very soothing, laid-back way about him that made me feel comfortable and never embarrassed.

Richardo, I noticed that you did not turn in your Geography homework this week. Is there a reason?

I composed myself. When I heard "geography" I knew. I took a deep breath,

But Mister Cherry, for two days I look for question box in the classroom and cannot find this box with questions for homework...so I not do it because...But where do jew keep this question box, please? And my name is said "Reecardo." "Reecardo."

Mr. Sherry's eyes opened widely. Then he smiled, parting open my Geography book and pointing to questions inside a red square on the pages with his index finger. *No, no Reechardo, the question boxes are not in the classroom, these are them, HERE, in the pages inside your book.* He pointed to the lines of a square printed around questions on the page.

Ahh, jew meen, the squares lines around on the questions? But these are not real boxes?

Yes, these are the question boxes.

I was puzzled. A box or *caja,* in Spanish is a three-dimensional object with four sides, a bottom and a top opening. Here, for two days I looked for three-dimensional boxes in the classroom, expecting to find envelopes with questions in them. What was all this craziness? A box is not a square... I thought. Then I laughed. *Los locos.*

Transitions

Slowly I began to work on my *Inglich.* I was always embarrassed to try to speak around kids I didn't know or didn't know me, because I was sure they would make fun of the way I spoke. Like Larry, down the street from where I lived.

La-aa-e-e-er-y! His mother would stand on the back deck of their aluminum-sided old house and scream his name for him to come in. Her voice sounded nearly as shrill as the Fire Drill siren in School No.9. The kids in our neighborhood always laughed hysterically when she did this. They said something about he and his family talking funny, that they were from the south and moved to New Jersey. I couldn't tell if Larry spoke funny or not, so I thought, if they thought he spoke funny, what did they think about how I spoke?

Yer' nuthin' but a Speeeak, hain't you? But do yew speak Cuban? When are yew gonna lern sum' English? That was Larry. So, I stayed away from him. *Loco from the south.*

I found out that they had cartoons on TV. At the time my cousin Carlos used to love to watch a cartoon series named *Hercules.* I had heard of Hercules and this was a superhero type of cartoon.

I am Herrrkulees! Great Zeus!

Hercules' voice sounded very self-assured, and he spoke slowly, not like people spoke in New Jersey. So, I decided to start repeating everything I heard Hercules say on the cartoons, not knowing what he was saying, but I figured this was a way to practice pronouncing *Inglich* correctly. *Don't worry, King Dorian. Let's go, Helen!* And like a parrot, I would repeat, *Don't worry, King Dorian. Let's go, Helen!* and so on. This of course, drove my cousin Carlos into a frenzy and he would stomp away from the TV really mad, especially when I would interrupt and ask him to translate what Hercules had said. He was so frustrated, he stopped watching the show, so I had the only TV in the house all to myself, repeating Hercules phrases out loud to no one.

Much to my amazement, within weeks I began to develop a really good ear for listening to people speaking English. *Mister Cherry* didn't speak New Jersey English and he spoke not so fast like everyone at school, so it became easier to listen to him. I wondered if he was from another part of the country or whether he maybe watched Hercules cartoons also. *But definitely not from Learrrry's South,* I thought. As time went by, I even began to notice that Larry did speak differently than most kids in New Jersey.

Crossed Signals

I distinctly remember the afternoon of November 22, 1963. Mr. Sherry stopped mid-sentence after another teacher burst into our class saying something about a disaster.

You've got to turn on the news, she said in a hurried way.

Mr. Sherry seemed startled, and several of the students began to talk excitedly. He reached into his desk drawer and pulled out a small transistor radio, turned it on to the news. I could not understand what was being said, only something about the police being on alert. I heard the word "emergency." Meanwhile, almost everyone in the class seemed to be talking, several students stood up and scuttled towards the windows, trying to peek out as if something bad was about to start happening outside.

It was a dreary, cloudy, and grey day. Although I could see the naked branches of the tips of some trees outside, they seemed like in a fog, in and out of focus. I went by the by the window as well to see about the commotion. I was shocked at what I saw.

Mr. Cherry! Mr. Cherry... Eeet is Es-nowin' outside! Look eett is Es-nowin'! I repeated, in what I thought was my best

Hercules accent. The class went quiet. Suddenly, everyone had their eyes on me...

Yes, it is snowing outside Reechardo, but the President of the United States has just been shot with a gun in Texas, and he could die... said Mr. Sherry, in a muted tone of voice.

Then I realized that the disaster was not about a snowstorm. The class was horrified. How stupid can one feel? I wanted to run and crouch beneath my desk, cover my head so no one could see me, nuclear-bomb-drill-style. I was ashamed and embarrassed, but I must admit, that seeing those thousands of fluffy, white snowflakes wafting down from the sky, some hitting the glass on the windows and disintegrating into water droplets was one of the most beautiful things I had seen since arriving in grimy New Jersey. That night the city was blanketed with snow, and I would find out from my cousin Carlos that President Kennedy died. Other than the snow, how was this different than people getting murdered in Cuba? This would happen all the time back home in Matanzas before we left. So why did we have to leave?

In those days of adjustment, I sometimes would cry when I was by myself. I felt so out of place in New Jersey. I kept thinking about Juanito's farm, and mangoes, and my dog Yuti. What were they doing in Matanzas? The snowflakes had been pretty, but the cold was not for me, and neither was the getting dark at five p.m. every night, and I thought if the president of the United States could get killed, just like that, by some stranger, this wasn't much different than Cuba. So why did we leave?

Detour

Days after President Kennedy was killed, Mrynn and I were taken out of our class and escorted to an empty classroom.

Mr. Sherry and a lady whom I didn't recognize came in with paper booklets and sheets with circles and letters in rows and columns. She handed one booklet to me and one to Mrynn and we each got two sharpened pencils and a sheet with the circles in it and space for us to print our names at the top. Mr. Sherry explained we would have about two hours and that we should look at the questions and drawings on the book carefully and mark the best answers on the sheet with the circles, filling each circle. He explained things again, as if he wasn't sure we understood what to do. We were separated by two rows. I looked at Mrynn and she looked at me, both somewhat puzzled that it was only the two of us that were being given this "test."

The lady stayed in the room to observe us. She had a stopwatch. *You must neither look over at each others' work nor speak to each other. If you need to use the rest room, raise your hand, turn your answer sheet upside down.*

I had no idea what she was talking about. Who was this woman? Were we in some kind of trouble?

Mr. Sherry had left us there. A couple of hours later, the lady said out loud, *Time is up! Close your booklets and put your pencils down, place your answer sheets inside the booklet.* She startled us the way she talked. We handed the booklets and sheets back to the lady after she clicked her stopwatch, She escorted us back to our class. We never heard anything about what this test was for. We never heard anything at all, whether we passed it, or what our grade was. This time I knew it wasn't just me. Mrynn was thinking the same thing. *Los locos.*

Derailment

Fast forward to 1965. I started school at North Bergen High School on Hudson Boulevard, which they just re-named "Kennedy Boulevard." A brand-new school, glossy bright linoleum floors, very nice-smelling and with large windows that opened. There was *grass* and there were pretty trees around the building. This was better than School No. 9, and thankfully Mrynn and I were in several classes together, except for maybe shop class, because girls didn't take shop.

Mr. Sahagian, our mathematics teacher, and assistant Bruins football coach pulled Mrynn and me aside one day after class and asked,

Tell me...I don't understand why you and Mrynn are in this class. I mean this class is for slow learners and for kids who have trouble with school. You seem bored. Are you having other problems?

The truth was, we were beyond bored in most of our classes. I zipped through my homework every night in no time, especially now that my *Inglich* was improving (thanks to Hercules) and I didn't have to translate things back and forth in English/Spanish. I think Mrynn and I both felt the same way. We didn't know why we were put in our classes. Everything seemed so easy. I wondered if I belonged in the tenth grade and maybe so did Mrynn...

Mr. Sahagian walked us down the hallway to the Counseling Office. We waited in the lobby and he went into Mrs. Marion's office probably to speak to her about our classes. She stood up and began looking through a file cabinet, pulled out two file folders and began to look through them. The door was partially open and I could hear and see them both talking.

*Hmm...*Mrs. Marion seemed puzzled. *Only thing I can think of is their non-English speakers' status.* She leafed back through a couple of pages, then she paused, and showed Mr. Sahagian.

Wait...this must be it... Low IQ. She said.

What? This can't be right! Sahagian turned and stretched

his head out the door of Mrs. Marion's office. *Do you remember taking an "IQ" test when you were at Horace Mann?*

Mrynn and I looked at each other.

What's an eye cute test? I asked.

"I. Q." It's a test to check how smart or intelligent you are. They give you a book with questions and shapes and diagrams, then they ask you questions and you put the answers on a sheet of paper where you fill in little circles with a pencil...do you remember taking a test like that? Asked Mr. Sahagian.

I wanted to laugh, then I remembered. Yes! That day when Mr. Sherry took us out of a room and gave us the booklets. And we sat for two hours and the lady with the stopwatch took them back and we never heard or knew what this test was for.

Mr. Sahagian seemed angry, like he was about to explode.

This is just wrong, he shook his head from side to side, then looked at Mrs. Marion.

These kids couldn't even speak English, for Chrissake! Really? They hadn't even been in this country for three months! He glared at Mrs. Marion. *You have got to take care of this problem right away!*

Mrs. Marion was subdued. The next morning, Mrynn and I were taken out of Mr. Sahagian's class and put in another class. We were also put in a different English class and a different Science class for the rest of the year. *Locos!*

Thanks to Mr. Sahagian, four years later, Mrynn and I would graduate from North Bergen High School in the top ten percent of our class and attend college.

23
PAPI AND ME

A sixteen-degree forecast for North Florida was about the only type of day one would dare wear a herring bone wool sports coat and not look out of place. As I peeled the plastic bag off the hanger and pulled it from the closet, I noticed the handkerchief in the breast pocket.

The prior summer, I had found myself consoling my despondent mother, helping make funeral arrangements and sorting through my dead father's belongings. He had owned the jacket for over thirty years, probably only wore it three or four times. Sporting hand-crafted leather buttons, wide lapels, and stitched lining, Papi boasted "about the thick and precise weave, that it was handmade in Scotland..." He had bought it on sale at Schlessinger's, paid cash for it. It was the only nice thing my father ever bought for himself since we came to America.

Forty-five years earlier we had become steeped in a not unfamiliar trajectory for refugees, ten adults and six cousins crammed into "the uncle's house in New Jersey" and cozily sharing a single bathroom-one sink, one toilet. Since our having left Cuba, Papi worked temporarily as a dishwasher at Steak-n-Shake, then leveraging his 30-year experience as a grocer, he was hired as head cashier and bag boy in someone's Latin market. Every day, he stood at the bus stop at Bergenline and 85th. We had no car. He opened Kiko's Market six days a week, worked on his feet 12-13 hours each day for a not-to-boast-about hourly wage. The owner made good money. My mother, a former school principal in Cuba, worked the graveyard shift cleaning bedpans and surgical instruments in a community hospital. She and Papi saw each other during the week like passing ships, and during weekends we spent time together as a family. That would be the rhythm of our lives in New Jersey for several years.

My father thrived on the simplicity of life. I remembered a few months after we arrived in the US, when on a bus to southern New Jersey we passed a cornfield. He stood up from his seat marveling at the orderly rows, the tall stalks, the deep green leaves. I think it reminded him of the remote farm where he grew up, with four younger brothers and two sisters which he ultimately left behind when we came to the United States. He was mortified and greatly embarrassed, when in his excitement, looking out the back window, the bus driver barked out loud in New-Joisyish English *Hey, you! Sit down bac dare!* Papi didn't understand what the man was saying and was greatly embarrassed and offended as other passengers looked up. It wouldn't be the last time he would be embarrassed about not speaking or understanding English. Despite efforts by me and my brother to teach him, he struggled. It was hard for a man in his mid-fifties with barely an eighth-grade education to learn a new language. He couldn't understand why people became frustrated when he struggled with his *Inglich,* which made him that much more self-conscious. For almost 10 years he depended on one of us to accompany him to the bank to translate when he deposited his paychecks.

My father had immaculate handwriting and even with a disabling lack of sensation in his fingers that he could no longer button his shirts, he wrote often to our family back home. We, in turn, rarely heard from them. When I inquired, Papi proposed that the mail delivery there was poor or that they couldn't afford the stamps to write us or that the government intercepted the letters. There was probably some truth in all his explanations, but I suspect these were in part a justification, his way of coping with unrequited replies. I think he felt responsible that they stayed behind and that he left, duty-bound, with his immediate family. I recalled him one evening sitting pensively by a window, with a paper pad on his lap, while he wrote to his siblings in Cuba. It was before Christmas, an urban-grey New Jersey day, and it was snowing heavily. It must have been painful for him to be away from his siblings, longing for the Cuban sun, and knowing he might never see them again.

Papi was ecstatic one day when early in my senior year of high school he approached me with a proposal.

Ricar, he said, *If I save enough money, you and I could be partners and we could buy our own bodega for ourselves.*

Although dreading my response, I had to be frank and told him that what I really wanted was to go to college and eventually study medicine. Facial muscles betrayed his disappointment, and with a forced smile and a deflated nod, he acknowledged my response, never to bring up the topic again.

My father continued to work until he was 72, when his knees no longer allowed him to stand for long periods of time. He helped me through college, and then through medical school. Several years ago, he stood beside me for a photo when I was honored by students I taught as Professor of Medicine at a school where I eventually established myself as a senior faculty member.

The summer he died I had sorted through his personal belongings. I folded the jacket and put it in my suitcase along with his old wallet and his penknife. Inside a well-creased envelope, postmarked May 1973, was a five-page letter I had written him thirty-four years earlier upon graduating from college. Written longhand in Spanish, I had detailed how much I appreciated him, and all the sacrifices he made for me and for our family. I told him that I loved him, that I hoped I could make him proud of me some day. I also let him know that every time I wrote out my middle name (his first name), I thought of him. It was the only letter I found in his belongings. I flew back to Florida.

On this cold February morning, months later, while getting dressed to make hospital rounds with my residents, I slipped on Papi's wool jacket. It fit, looked, and felt right. I noted a little hard bulge over the breast pocket. When I pulled the handkerchief from the pocket, a peppermint wrapped in plastic fell onto the bed.

Standing in front of the mirror, wearing my father's jacket, and holding the peppermint and handkerchief in each hand, I chuckled. Papi always insisted that it was impolite to cough in public, and he never forgot to remind us that if we went out, we should always take a mint in case we felt the urge to cough... and yes, in the event we coughed, we should always have a handkerchief to cover our mouth.

Being a lung specialist, many of my patients struggle with incessant coughs. How ironic was it to have found myself, so ensconced in the academia of it all, that I had forgotten all about peppermint and coughs.

My father had simple likes, but he was also a complex man. He carried his emotions deeply and quietly. Complaining about the hardness of life was never part of his vocabulary. He was well-liked by the countless customers he served as a grocer and businessman for over sixty years of his profession, both in Cuba and in Kiko's market. It was not unusual for me to see my father interact with strangers over the years, even those who could not understand his broken English, and universally they always seemed to find my father likeable. At home, Papi rarely showed exuberance in his emotions, except for those times his granddaughters tickled him mercilessly. In my fifty-seven years around him I never saw my father cry. I am sure he cried, but if he did, it was not in his nature to shed tears publicly. This was not something I inherited from him. I wondered sometimes if things between Papi and me might have been different. We might have had a great father-and-son grocery business.

As I stepped into my car on the way to work, I conjured a hint of his Old Spice aftershave and I could almost feel the warmth and familiar grip of his two muscular arms wrapped around me from behind, just like he used to do when I was little.

I approached the on-ramp on the highway. Looking in the rearview mirror, I thought about my middle name.

24
UNA COINCIDENCIA

I had been fired from my job at the N.J. Office of Unemployment after only one week. The supervisor there said I did a great job and that although it helped greatly that I was bilingual, and all my coworkers liked me, he had to let me go because I wasn't a U.S. Citizen. I told him that in my application I clearly stated I was a green-card-holding, permanent U.S. Resident. But it was to no avail. He apologized for the bureaucratic snafu. Regulations stated I had to be a U.S. Citizen.

Well, that was my situation. No job for the summer in between my second and third year of college, and too late in the season to try to find something that paid decently. So I took whatever was available, and began working as a security guard at the then exclusive designer, Jonathan Logan's Clothing factory in Union City New Jersey. I wore a white short sleeve shirt, black tie, and dark navy pants. I even wore a badge, but no radio and thankfully, no weapons. In a glass partition at the entrance to the factory, I worked the day shift, 7-3 pm. My job was to check in and direct any buyers or visitors that came to the factory but most importantly to make sure the seamstresses (most of them middle aged Asian or Latinas) did not sneak out any of the expensive slinky designer dresses they worked so hard all day to sew. (Word had it from the management that the factory "lost" 20-40 expensive dresses per week, attributed to employee theft.) It was embarrassing for me that I had to have the employees open their purses and lunch sacs every day on the way out but I suspected it was even more demeaning for them that I put them through this humiliation after a long and miserable day at the noisy factory, when in fact it was common knowledge that the "disappearances" took place at the dock when an extra dress or two were tagged on to the racks upon loading.

Señora, could you open up your bag so I can take a look, please?

The lady looked at me politely, hesitated, and after giving me a half smile, she turned briefly to her coworker behind her. They both giggled.

Por favor, open your bolsa? I pointed to the purse.

I was aghast to find a hairy looking brown bundle rolled up inside her bag. My demeanor immediately changed to security guard mode. *Please, Señora, I need to have you empty the contents of your purse on the table.*

At first, I thought it was a piece of fur, then perhaps a dead animal. I was surprised when the woman took the item out, unfolded it and with both hands held it up to me: a man's toupeé! She and her coworkers exploded in nervous laughter. I felt I had been set up and was definitely had.

The woman then said to me, apologetically and in a very thick Spanish accent: *Pleese... It is the* hair *peluca of the boss of my husband and it was a leetle broken on the border so I brought it in to fix it with the good sewing machine. I do not want to make no trouble...*

Another time a very demure-looking employee who was probably in her late fifties saw the cover of a book I had splayed on my table as she walked by. It was a Spanish edition of *Laberintos* by Nobel Prize recipient Jorge Luis Borges. The woman stopped, cleared her throat, and said very politely,

Excuse me, but do 'jew spik Espanish?

Claro que sí, soy Cubano. Of course, I'm Cuban, I replied.

She had a look of disbelief. *Dat' is bery funny...but 'jew don't look Cuban,* she replied, this time in broken English. *I 'an Cuban too!*

Que bueno. I replied. *Are you Católica?*

Jes,' and then she reached into her blouse and pulled out a small medal of the *Virgen of El Cobre,* patron saint of Cuba, held it between thumb and index finger to my face. I nodded. Then I replied, in a very respectful tone, *That's funny, but you don't look Catholic!* We laughed.

Except for the occasional humorous interludes with the seamstresses, and getting to eat lunch with the loading dock guys, and for the times when some really slick, great-looking movie-star type women came in to visit the factory with some of the head honchos, the everyday routine of my security-guarding was beyond monotonous. But it was a job. I brought in books I anticipated listed as required reading for the fall semester so I could read while I had down time during the day. And I had plenty of down time. I was payed $6.75 an hour, but the building was air-conditioned and at least I wasn't loading trucks off Tonelle Avenue or mowing yards or waxing cars, or otherwise humping it in the heat like most of my neighborhood friends. Come 3pm I still had a good chunk of the day left to go and play tennis or just hang around outside, so it ended up being a tolerable situation. The highlight of my day every day was to hand off keys and log book to the evening security guard, just so I could be out on time.

The evening security guard was probably around the same age as me. The way he acted, it looked like this was his year-round job. All summer it was like we were passing ships. He came in around 3pm, and I signed out to him by 3:10 or so, in a hurry to beat traffic on Kennedy Boulevard. He seemed like a nice guy but I never did small talk or engage him in conversation because I was always in a hurry to get out. I didn't even know his name.

The summer was coming to an end and I would be leaving my job in a week to head up to college for my junior year. My last Friday afternoon came, and when the evening security guard came to relieve me, we struck a conversation and I decided to stay and chat with him, feeling guilty that short of cursory handoffs we hadn't gotten to talk to each other all summer. I told him my name was Ricardo and we exchanged platitudes, that it was my last day and I would be heading back to college the next week. We continued our conversation.

Ricardo. He paused. *So where are you from?*

I was born in Cuba and came to New Jersey in 1963. And you?

That's funny, I was born in Cuba, too! He said. *But how come you don't have an accent?*

Well, you don't have an accent either. And you don't look Cuban.

That's because my parents were from Lebanon.

Really? So, what city did you live in when you lived in Cuba?

Oh, you probably never heard of it. A little town named Placetas, in the province of Santa Clara.

I couldn't believe what I was hearing. My uncles, both doctors, lived in Placetas, where they started a clinic and small hospital. Yes, it was a small town. I spent two summers with my cousin in Placetas and had great memories of the place.

Placetas. Yes, I know where that is. Did you know "The Clinica Moderna"?

Yes. I lived around the corner from the clinic, in a green stucco house. He acted surprised. *Really, you know Placetas?*

It had been over ten years and although I did not recognize him, after he told me his name, I began to think hard if I had ever met him. I couldn't match the way he looked to any memory, and after all, he was over six feet tall and very muscular, his voice was that of a man, and he sported a short, preppy type haircut-not exactly your basic Cuban phenotype.

Did you by any chance know a girl named Yamilé?

Yes, of course. She is my sister! And my father owned a warehouse in town, he said, rather surprised. Yamilé was a beautiful olive-skinned girl, long thick wavy hair, very dark eyebrows and eyelashes and gorgeous round green eyes. My cousin Carlos had a deep crush on her.

In Placetas, Uncle Evaristo's house was directly across from the clinic building. Us kids would sit on the front porch and watched people on the street, throwing rocks at neighborhood chickens and stray dogs, and sometimes playing catch on the empty lot next door. The lot was grassy and crossing the property, there was a bare path where grass no longer grew because people always trampled the trail as a shortcut. Bored, one day me, my cousin and his friends decided to play a prank and we dug a hole along the trail on the trampled path. The hole was a good two feet wide and another two feet deep. We criss-crossed it with thin branches, put cardboard over the branches, and then sprinkled some soil over the cardboard, just enough to cover the opening over the hole and to restore the look of the dirt path. We carried the extra soil away and sat on the porch, waiting for someone to cut through the diagonal path.

Back at Jonathan Logan's, it suddenly came to me. I took a chance and asked my security guard colleague: *Do you by any chance remember an empty lot next to the house across from the clinic?*

Yes I do.

And do you remember walking across a path through the middle of the lot one day, and falling into a hole?

Yes, but how do you know that? He looked like he'd seen a ghost.

Because I'm the one that dug that hole!

The following week on my three-hundred-mile drive back to college I got to thinking about my summer and I reminisced about my childhood in Placetas. What had started out as a potentially disappointing job situation led me to a place where I would have least considered under the wildest of circumstances to have a serendipitous opportunity to reconnect with my past. Was this a coincidence? I should think not. It was more like a gift I wasn't expecting, an unusual connecting of dots in a surreal matrix of time.

I had finished *Laberintos* the night before heading back to school. In this book of essays and short stories Borges wrote a magical tale "*Funes the Memorious.*" Following an accident, the protagonist awoke paralyzed, but with intense and very rich recollections about his life memories. Funes could remember with great clarity every single word he ever said, when he said it, what every window he passed or object he had ever seen looked like. This great recall ability became a maddening curse for Funes, who felt pressured that he would never have time to recall all his childhood memories by the hour of his death. Was my reading *Laberintos* also a coincidence?

25
REMEMBERING TO FORGET

For the first year since arriving in New Jersey, although I understood why we had to leave, from a purely selfish point of view, I really resented leaving Cuba. I kept hoping that like my parents had said, once Castro and his Revolution were over, *things would get better in Cuba.* We would have a free country with democracy like the United States and everything would be ok for us to return to our house, to our friends and of course, I would be able to get my dog, Yuti back.

Now I was living in someone else's house in New Jersey with no privacy. I didn't have my own room. I didn't have a desk. I didn't have peace and quiet, except during sleep, or if I went out of the house to the park on 85th street and Bergenline Avenue where I would sometimes sit on a park bench and watch the old Italian guys play bocce as the squirrels romped in the branches above. That, and watching the blue jays and starlings rummage for food scraps on the park garbage bins constituted my communing with nature. There was never any "true quiet." The urban noises of cars, honking horns, traffic, construction, and police car sirens were inescapable.

The hardness of living in our neighborhood in New Jersey made my yearning to be back in Matanzas that much stronger. It was especially bad during the first winter. After a couple of snowball fights, making a snowman, and sliding down the hill on my cousin's sled in the park, the thrill and novelty of winter faded fast. Having to shovel a half foot of snow off the stoop, clearing the cracked, often uneven sidewalks with a snow shovel became a chore. It was not at all like the holly branches with red bows and snowy cabins out in the woods, pretty and idyllic like the Christmas cards portrayed. Shoveling the sooty, dog waste-infested snow from the sidewalk onto the street was not allowed in our town, so we piled it on the curb, often blocking the doors of parked cars. Shoveling snow late at night when the temperature dipped below freezing, especially on school nights, was onerous. It was either that, or get up at five, shovel hard, sweat, undress, fight for the one shower in the one-bathroom house, which usually meant skipping breakfast and still be late for school.

A man in our neighborhood died of a massive heart attack while shoveling snow. We often offered to shovel some of the neighbors' sidewalks, especially the little old Italian widows, and there were many of those living in our neighborhood. I couldn't in good conscience imagine one of those sweet old women in their black dress, black stockings, black kerchief headwear and black shoes suffer the indignity of pushing a snow shovel and slipping on the ice. I began shoveling walks for some other neighbors and it was a good way to earn some money. It was backbreaking work, and getting cold and wet was most unpleasant, especially with the good quality winter wear I didn't have. Sometimes I would come into the house to take my boots and jacket off and find dogshit on my gloves as I grabbed onto the soles of my rubber boots. Great! Half-frozen dogshit on the boots, now smeared in my gloved, then ungloved, frozen hands and only winter coat. A veritable winter wonderland in the city.

I became acutely aware that my parents didn't have it easy in New Jersey. When we first arrived, papi originally tried to find work so he could help support us. Yes, we had a roof over us at my uncle's house, but papi felt he needed to contribute to paying our share of rent, food, and utilities for the collective. We were imposing on our relatives enough as it was, all of us crammed into that house. I don't know how we managed sometimes. They say familiarity breeds contempt, but we adjusted, nevertheless.

I suppose that most people would find that four families living elbow to elbow, sharing one bathroom and one kitchen in the same household might feel intrusive, uncomfortable, if not at times unbearable. It did. But this was the rule rather than the exception for many immigrants. It was mostly out of financial necessity, but on the plus side, it gave us a centered sense of community, of pulling and scraping towards the same goal together. We all contributed to and shared literally from the same pot. Nothing was thrown away. Fix it, mend it, or see if anyone else can use it as last resort. All for one and one for all. I found it ironic that this situation of communal living, as old as the evolution of man, when corrupted by people greedy for power, seeking to control the masses, was the very "communism" that put humans in such peril that it drove them to flee places like Berlin, Prague, Warsaw, and now, Matanzas.

Thus was the power of communal living: unprompted, my cousin Carlos took it upon himself to scan the Hudson Dispatch and Jersey Journal for jobs listings that might suit someone who couldn't speak the language, had no drivers' license, and could walk to work. He found an opening advertised at a nearby diner. My cousin Carlos took papi there to translate and inquire about work.

Success. Papi got the job as a dishwasher at a diner on Hudson Boulevard. But it only lasted five days. He couldn't speak English, and it wasn't the physical difficulty of the actual job, but the working conditions. The near-nothing hourly pay with no benefits didn't help. But it was a job. He didn't have gloves to wear at work and couldn't ask where to get them. That first day, he came home with scalded hands from the steam and from scrubbing pots and pans in the hot dishwater. He was finally given a pair of elbow-high rubber gloves but almost overnight after wearing them for a full shift, he developed a horrible rash on both hands and arms that wouldn't heal so that he could not physically do the work required. Because of the sores in his arms and hands, he wasn't allowed to return to work until they cleared. Catch 22. He left the diner never to return to dishwashing, and a couple of weeks later would take a job as a glorified cashier/stock-clerk/bag boy in a Latin bodega in Union City, working 12 hours a day, six days a week, taking the same bus from the same bus stops where he got on and off for the next 35 winters until he retired because his seventy plus year-old-knees could no longer hold.

Through the years, I would sometimes overhear my uncles and parents talk about the things going on in Cuba, like the government takeover of all private foreign industrial enterprises and how many companies like Coca Cola, United Sugar, etc. ended up pulling out of the country altogether. They spoke about how food and basic necessities had gotten even harder to come by. Tío Evaristo joked that the cardboard ration cards were designed to be used in place of the toilet paper once one could no longer buy toilet paper using the ration cards. My uncles also talked about how the Pedro Pan flights of children leaving Cuba to Miami had been discontinued since we left. My uncles on papi's side had to relinquish the family's small farm to the *Movimiento de la Revolucíon* as their land was engulfed by a government agrarian cooperative. Displaced farmers had no choice but to move to town. They became like ducks out of water. But, so what? I didn't see the relevance of cooperatives and farmers in Cuba, and solidarity of the people there as a concern to me. As a teen-ager with undeveloped frontal lobes, I was more worried about looming, life-emergent issues like the sore, horrible-looking pimples on my face, the living with hand-me-down clothes, being ridiculed by my classmates, like the day Mr. Sherry asked me to talk to the class about my experiences in Cuba.

This is how it happened: As I developed more courage with my English, one day I spoke in class about the "Measle Crisis." I told the class *that there were many Russian Measles all over the island...*The kids were howling. Someone in class might have even asked me at the time why they didn't have vaccines in Cuba, which I thought seemed like an odd question. That is, until *Mr. Cherry* kindly interjected, trying to clarify that he thought I was talking about "missiles" rather than about an epidemic of infectious disease. Looking back, it must have been really hilarious. Well, I didn't think it was funny back then and I am sure that Hercules would have strongly objected to my pronunciation of the term for the projectiles used to deliver nuclear weapons.

After the first couple of years since our arrival, while struggling to find my balance, I began to focus more on just trying to survive going to school, on doing better to help my family, and I probably chose, semi-consciously, to not think about Juanito, or

Yuti, or mango trees. Or about Cuba, period. All that stuff of my childhood had become like an itchy scab, and every time I picked at it, it would only re-bleed and not heal. I dealt with that past by remembering to forget. I finally reckoned that although mami and papi kept the enthusiasm, "that one day soon we would go back," this would never really come to pass. We were in New Jersey, to stay: permanent residents. We should be thankful and glad. The prophecy from the old guy with top hat the red white and blue uniform from the cover of the magazine staring at me in the toilet that morning of our first October in New Jersey was coming through.

During my selective blindness about the goings-on in Cuba over the ensuing several years, I worried instead about imminently personal issues, like whether I would be drafted to fight (and die) in some napalm-scorched rice paddy in Viet Nam. In high school I began having very good success on the track team and my *Inglich* had now transitioned nicely into relatively smooth, conversational English. I was also doing well in school. Mami helped me buy an acoustic guitar for $10 and I began to teach myself how to play it. I began to listen to the Beatles, Van Morrison, Bob Dylan, The Four Tops, and Aretha Franklin. I also listened to the music of Celia Cruz, Chucho Valdèz, and Los Muñequitos at home. I became oblivious to external current events, like the reality that some of my school classmates from Matanzas could have eventually ended up as one or several of the 1500 killed, wounded, or missing, or of the 5000 or so who deserted while serving in the Soviet-led and Cuban-aided People's Armed Forces for the Liberation of Angola in the African continent.

Years later, while I was in college, mami had mentioned that one of the most outstanding students that she taught in

Aguacate, (this was years before I ever guest-played in their marching band), had become a prominent officer in the ranks of the Cuban army of the revolution. He, like many Cubans, had been a believer and supporter of the liberation of Cuba from the likes of tyrants like Batista, but apparently became dissatisfied when Ché Guevara and company steered the government towards communism instead of democracy. Mami told me she had read in one of the Miami exile newspapers that her former student had been court-martialed and sent to *El Presidio,* at Isla de Pinos (Isle of the Pines), where he eventually died of pneumonia and starvation. *Isla de Pinos* is an island of nine hundred square miles of pines and marble quarries which sits just south off the coast of mainland Cuba and where *El Presidio* was located. In this infamous prison, atrocities involving political prisoners of the movement took place, off-shore, and out-of-sight of people in the mainland. The prison was shut down in 1967, and the island was euphemistically re-branded as *Isla de la Juventud* (Isle of Youth) where "educatíon of the young" and tourism have since flourished over the years. The prison was since declared a museum. A fellow Cuban, former prisoner on the island who eventually gained his freedom and came to the United States, tells me that although the paint on *El Presidio* may have flaked, and the walls have cracked, and despite the island's name change, ghosts will forever roam the island prison as a testament reminder to the suffering of many who were captive there.

During my third year in medical school, the news about a mass exodus of Cubans arriving at the shores of *Cayo Hueso* (Key West) and Miami during the Mariel boat lift got my attention. What I remembered from the news blurbs is that Castro had allowed exit to anyone on the island who wished to leave in order "to reunite with their families abroad," no questions asked. The rumors from the Miami exile community news were that Castro used the Mariel boatlift as a ploy to decompress his prisons and insane asylums, as well as to rid the island of groups of people who might not be fully "in synch" with the ideals of the revolutionary movement. Rather than welcoming, many established Miami expatriates resented the new refugees, claiming these were mostly criminals who would give the Cubans a bad name and worsen crime and corruption in Miami, making it bad for all "us" Cubans in the United States. *Yes, be careful with those Marielitos, you know, especially the ones with the heavy tatoos, they will break into your house, give you drugs, rape your abuelita and then kill you dead! Maricones comunistas arrepentidos!* That was the sentiment of many Miami Cubans about the Mariel "boat people."

Through the years, papi tried to maintain contact with his family in Matanzas, mainly with two of his surviving brothers who stayed behind, and his sister, Hilda, the baby of the family. The mail communication was poor if near non-functional. For every ten or twenty letters my father would write, he might receive one reply from his family. It was obvious that many of the envelopes had been tampered with and resealed. But they would write in code words, and it was clear from the tone of the letters, that my uncles feared being watched as to what they said or did. Most of the news about people in Matanzas would come from people who had left the island as *balseros* paddling homemade rafts through the Florida Straits or from those who had left through Spain, came to Miami, and knew someone who knew someone else and then the information would be shared. A whole host of Cuban exile periodicals were also a great source of news, rumors, and gossip. Mami learned that one of my friends from *el barrio* left Cuba through Spain and eventually settled in Miami. He was gunned down on the streets, and it was presumably drug-related. My father found out about his brother, Lolo's death several weeks after he passed, and it was by word of mouth. By now it had become much easier to remember my childhood as simple, with the Matanzas I knew as a child, minus all the political intrigue, which despite efforts to not pay mind to it, was impossible at times to ignore. I cultivated the practice of remembering to forget, thus allowing myself a safe harbor of denial. It would become my way of avoiding regrets and harping on what had been, realizing I could never get back my wonderful childhood.

In recent years, while my parents were still living, they both expressed at different times a desire to go back to the island and visit. I felt especially bad for papi, because I knew how much he missed the siblings he left behind. It was still not straightforward to arrange travel at that time, and trying to travel through Mexico with my dad who could barely walk because of severe degenerative arthritis of his knees and chronic heart failure was too precarious in my view to risk. A couple of years after papi died, during one of her lucid periods, mami also expressed she would like to go back and visit Matanzas. She always wondered what happened to our little house on *Calle Medio*, and she had told me that although at one time she was bitter and had the utmost contempt for what the communists did to ruin our lives and livelihoods, she thought that fifty years later, the majority of the people born on the island who were young, who had not grown up with the original Castro movement, had no perspective and were born into a repressive autocratic system and probably knew no better, and didn't have a choice. She thought they needed forgiveness and understanding rather than loathing. Mami was in fact wise in her assessment. But by this time, she had become very forgetful as well. My dad had died, and I didn't want to risk traveling with her in her state of poor physical and emotional health either. I realized that for both mami and papi, even late in life, well as they concealed their emotions through their life in the United States, unlike me, it would never be possible for them to remember to forget. I resolved to no longer forget and made myself a promise to return one day, as a proxy of sorts, and also with the hopes of tracking down Juanito's whereabouts in Matanzas.

26
THE LAST TWO BEATS

4,123,438,320.

In her 98 years on the planet that is how many times her heart might have beat. And I had the palm of my hand gently over her chest for the last two. Then...it stopped. Silence. No tactile sensation. No more breath. Just stillness. I was thankful. But it was a bittersweet exit, for it left a great void in my chest.

For those last seemingly interminable hours, my brother and I had lain on either side of her. On that old doughy mattress of hers, my brother and I prayed that somewhere in the depths of her unresponsiveness, she might have some awareness that her two sons, who just loved her so, would be beside her as promised.

She had just had her 98th birthday when the fever and the shortness of breath came and the confusion became worse. Agitation. Anxiety. Antibiotics. Oxygen. She never complained. She would open her eyes intermittently, and though gasping, she would manage a kind smile as she tugged at her oxygen cannula. Taking guppy breaths, she could barely sip water to keep her lips moist.

Control of her thoughts had left my mother years before, and despite disabling arthritis and memory lapses in large parts of her day, my mother had an admirable attitude. Even as her heart struggled during those last hours, and the white cells and inflammatory fluids slowly drowned her from within the air sacs in her lungs, she managed to rescue a smile.

It was spiritually crushing to know that this wonderful person who bore me, who took care of me as a baby, who nursed me, who stayed up with and held me during febrile hallucinations, who accepted my sour milk vomitus on her chest as a blessing and not an inconvenience, who saw me at my best as she sprayed my little curls with violet water and combed me gently, who never once flinched at her responsibility for my life and for what I would become, lay now deflated, expired, immotile, cold beneath her flowered quilt. Greatly relieved to know that she had lived well, at least my brother and I had the certainty of knowing that she had exited with her soul intact.

Ricardito...give the *little ducky some bread...*

I suspect that is what she might have been saying to me, if I had a speech balloon to fill into the tattered black and white photo of her. In it, she sat beside me on a blanket at Simpson Park in Matanzas that day, beside a pond. Two ducks approached. In the image she had something between her index finger and thumb that she was putting in my tiny outstretched hand. There was also a little bag of what looked like bread crumbs beside her skirt. Papi recalled I may have been just over a year old in that photograph. I had to have been wearing cloth diapers, because at the time that is all we had. Cloth diapers. If soiled or peed on, as I learned seven years later, when my brother René was a baby, cloth diapers had to be rinsed, hand-washed, bleached and boiled in a pot, then hung to dry in a clothesline, to be reused again. Diapers notwithstanding, mami had the drive to put me in a stroller, and walk to the *parque de los patos* (the ducks' park). We had no car. She was still nursing me. Simpson Park was many blocks from our house. And she was in essence by herself, with me and whoever took the photo. The photographer must have been one of my uncles, probably Uncle Migue, because we didn't own a camera and my father would not have known how to use one. Uncles, fathers, or grandfathers, like most men in Cuba, did not change diapers, they did not carry diaper bags, and they didn't push strollers, either. There were no plastic baggies then to store soiled diapers, no moist towelettes, no butt paste. The diapers were clipped on with safety pins. So mami was in essence all alone that day, absent the standby cameraman, taking the chance with me in a cloth diaper, just so we could be outside, she and I, on a blanket, so that we could experience the duckies together.

Several years later, one saturday morning a soft cool breeze flowed overhead as we sat by the patio.

Ricar, quieres pan y jugo! she asked. I loved washing down toasted Cuban bread and butter with gulps of fresh squeezed orange juice in the mornings, especially on weekends. As mami sliced the oranges and squeezed the pulp in the little glass-juicing bowl on the patio table, I looked up at my bedsheets as they flapped over us like peace flags on a battlefield. I couldn't wait for them to dry and for mami to take them off the clothesline, hoping no one else would see them.

Mis payamas tienen orina. (My pijamas are soaked with urine.) *No pude aguantar en la oscuridad...* (I couldn't hold it in and it was dark...)

I was six years old. It had been happening once a week or so, especially during school nights. Mami knew. She never asked questions. She never chastised. She would pull the sheets off my bed and I never actually saw her washing them, because she would shut the door to the bathroom and then come out with them, wrung out but still dripping wet, to hang on the patío clothesline. Never said a word to papi or not even to abuela. No one ever knew.

But I knew. I would bet none of the kids in my first-grade class at Irene Toland peed their beds at night. If papi ever found out, he would have probably punished me for it. So mami never said. She never told me it was weird. I guess living with my Tío Yayo and taking care of her brothers when they were little, and being a teacher maybe gave her a little patience. Besides, Tío Yayo would almost always pee his pants during his jerking epileptic fits, so mami was probably used to it, and she knew it wasn't his fault. Well, I didn't think then that this was my fault either. But I felt so guilty and like I was a bad person for wetting my bed. I never said. I just held it all in, until I couldn't—I suppose. But my *payamas* reliably betrayed me.

As a child, mami was sister and caretaker to four brothers, three of whom were younger than her, and one who suffered from epileptic fits that could come on at any time, day, or night. My mom had to grow up quickly. Abuela said she was a good student. She was quiet and respectful, except for the day, as abuela recounted, that my grandmother was called to the principal at mami's school. Mami was 11 years old.

Señora Silva, I have called you here today because your daughter, Rosa Lydia, has done a very bad thing. She refused to follow an order from her teacher, and this is why she was sent to my office.

According to abuela, some kids in the class had been talking and the teacher ordered the whole class to write *I shall not talk during class* one hundred times as punishment. But mami refused. Petite eleven-year-old, self-effacing Rosa Lydia Silva with the thick long dark curls and sweet smile was unmovable. She was sent to the principal immediately, where according to abuela, she lowered her head, broke down crying, crossed her hands over her knees and refused to speak. That is how abuela found her as she stepped into the *Oficina de el Director* that morning.

Señora, she must follow direcciones of her teacher and accept la sanción.

Little Rosa Lydia refused. She insisted she wasn't talking in class so she would not be punished for something she didn't do. Silence. The principal asked my abuela to leave the room. Ten or so minutes later, the door opened and she was released by the principal. With a subtle skip in her step, Rosa Lydia took abuela's hand and they went home for the day.

Que pasó con el Director? Asked abuela.

He told me I didn't have to write the punishment 100 times.

I promised I would write a poesía about our school instead.

Abuela told me the school *Director* liked the poem so much he had it set to music, and it became the official school song. That was but one of many poems and short stories my mother would write and publish through the remainder of her life.

In 1963 when we first arrived in *Neu Yersi*, Mami didn't speak English. She needed a job. Her Cuban credentials as teacher and school principal meant nothing in *Neu Yersi*. My aunt, who was a nurse, found her a job in Central Supply at a nearby hospital. Mami worked the graveyard shift. Her job antedated disposable hospital supplies, so besides bloodied surgical instruments she washed, rinsed, and autoclaved urinals, bedpans, vaginal speculums, anoscopes and other sundry soiled reusable hospital paraphernalia.

Working in Central Supply was not an occupatíon many people would envy. The graveyard shift crowd consisted of mostly middle-aged, divorced women, several whose work ethic could be understatedly characterized as just two or three notches below lazy. They made mami feel uncomfortable. A couple of the women routinely brought what mami thought was alcohol to work. But mami stayed to herself, she did her work, lay low. She became aware from their body language that some of her coworkers resented her for completing her assignments on time while they loafed.

One morning I was sick and stayed home from school. Mami came home from her work overnight. She was quiet and looked tired. I rarely ever saw her in the mornings because I would be gone to school by the time she got home from work.

Mami, estás bien? Are you sick? She looked up, shook her head from side to side, and burst out crying as she sat on the bed. I had never seen my mother cry with such sobs, her chest heaving. She could barely get her words out.

She described the people with whom she worked. She was humiliated because they made her wash all the urinals and empty the foul-smelling bedpans. Mami feared that although their supervisor was aware of the bad employee dynamics, the woman was too threatened by her employees' demeanor to intervene.

I am going to leave this work, I cannot tolerar this, Ricar. But I have fear that I have difficulty to find other job. But we need the money from my working also.

I put my arms around her, and tried to comfort her, but she was inconsolable.

But...did something else happen last night? Her cheek looked bruised. I became enraged. *Mami, tell me, what happened?*

Some woman I did not know, a supervisor I think, told me she need of help upstairs and that I must to help push a stretcher...to the basement. As she spoke, mami began to cry again, and in between sobs told me that while she was pushing the stretcher around a corner, she bumped her cheek onto a metal handle of some sort. She couldn't stop crying.

From the strong smell of urine, mami thought the stretcher was probably loaded with soiled urinals and other materials and that is why the side railings were up with a white sheet draped over the top. The woman whom she thought was a supervisor spoke in a demeaning tone, insisting mami remove the heavy stretcher from the hallway on the ward. Feeling pressured, she did as she was told. The elevator jolted as it touched down on the basement level. With the jarring, a human foot protruded from one end as the sheet covering the stretcher shifted. Alone with what she then realized was a dead patient on the stretcher, inside the elevator, horrified her. She tried desperately to push the buttons but the door would not open. Mami became hysterical, and when she finally found the morgue, as she went around the corner she must have misstepped and struck her face on a metal cart in the hallway.

After the ordeal, it became clear that the woman whom mami assumed was a "supervisor" from upstairs was a friend of the coworkers. The women had deliberately put her up to this horrible sick prank. They laughed and mocked her. There was no one to turn to. My mother was at the very lowest rung of an unskilled worker ladder. But despite her humiliatíon, she never quit. And she never complained. She said she couldn't. At the time I could not understand why. But ask any underdog immigrant and they would know why she acted the way mami did under those circumstances.

When I went away to college, six hours away, and then through four years of medical school, mami would often write me. I would call home weekly. Her meticulous hand-written letters were inspiring and full of hope. At times she included little poems she had written. During my collect calls to her, I would sometimes pour out my stresses and troubles, like when I fretted about being drafted to Viet Nam during my first year of college, or when I thought I might lose my scholarship. She would usually hear me out, never judging or telling me what to do.

Yew haf to haf patience, Ricar. Let things go sontimes' and they work out. Paciencia and faith. That was her mantra. It became my spiritual balm.

Years later, during my internship I met a wonderful person at work. I told mami about her during a phone call, that I had fallen for all her wonderful qualities, but that I worried this woman might not feel the same way about me as I felt about her.

Yew haf to haf patience, Ricar. Let things go sontimes' and they work out...

Leslie and I would be married several months later. My wife has many of the wonderful qualities I saw in my mother growing up: she is a strong, independent woman, smart, creative, no-nonsense, and most of all, physically and emotionally beautiful. My father, my uncles and my grandfather may have taught me how to be manly, but my mother taught me how to be a man, a husband, and a father to two girls.

4,123,438,320 beats. If my mother could speak from beyond, she would probably say that those last two beats were but a comma and a period aptly placed in the final sentence of a well-lived life.

27
SPIC

Spic /*spik*/ ***noun*** (Informal-Offensive) *A contemptuous term for a Spanish-speaking person from Central or South America or the Caribbean.* *

*Origin of SPIC (Urban Dictionary): when a Hispanic person was to be arrested and no one could understand anything they were saying, the cops would write **S***panish* **P***erson* **I***n* **C***ustidy* on the police report.

I am looking at the black-and-white photograph on my high school ID. I was 17, and I can hardly believe it was me. I started my second year in high school, still suffering with my *Inglich*, shamed by the gross pimples on my face, dealing with the inconvenient reality of living as a *refugiado*: like still sleeping in the same 14x16 room with my parents and 10-year-old brother, like wearing someone else's clothes from the Catholic charity of a church I was too embarrassed to attend for fear someone sitting in the pew behind me would see me wearing *their* sweater. I struggled with accepting that the premise/promise of my returning to Matanzas "in a couple of years" was a fading fantasy that Mami and Papi made up in order for all of us to get by while still retaining hope that we might make it through if we worked hard in this country, and of course, only for a little while, until Castro et al. moved on-which they didn't. By now I hardly ever thought about Yuti, and didn't even know if he might still be alive. It made me sad to think about my friends back in Matanzas. So, I tried not to.

I had a temper then, a *bona fide encabronado* I was. One could say I figuratively cracked and smashed the portrait of the artist as an angry young man in many pieces, and on several occasions. I don't think back then I could have ever imagined where I would end up. It was like at one time I became the *Don Quijote* for the downtrodden in Union City. What others had in lack of self-righteousness I made up for with frustration at "*el sistema*." I let it all roil inside of me. I tried to tell myself all these years that anger was a destroyer, that it eroded the lining of the stomach and burned it with acid, that it constricted the coronary arteries, that it made one ugly, and that *in altitudine sua*, it pushed people away. I just thought people who knew me might wish to know I had worked for five decades on this bad habit. I no longer went to bed angry at anyone anymore. I also discovered that it was possible to make "It is what it is" my mantra without betraying my sense of social justice. It would have been useful for me to know that when I couldn't change "*el sistema*," going around it might have served me better and even saved me some wrinkles. I had also finally learned to attack windmills strategically.

I had little patience then. As for patience now, I have watched many river rocks. They didn't start out smooth but many survived the current and found their place. I had to be the best intermediate hurdler in the state of New Jersey. Close, but not quite. I tore my hamstring on three occasions. Were all the bronze medals worth it? Absolutely. I realized that not being first was less important than not doing my best, and this taught me humility. I had paid dearly for the sequela of overzealousness over the years in almost all life spheres (except love and faith) and I am glad that my virulence for love and my dedication to faith never waned.

It took me a while but now I learned to know my limitations. But my *extranjero* spirit of daring, that *chispa* of passion intermittently fired up my cortex, egged me on from time to time, begged me to paddle faster and harder, because even when I didn't see them I knew the sharks were always going to be there, beneath the surface and around me.

My mind said *I'm still a sophomore*, my body disagrees. And so, in these days of my second chapter I paddled and bird-watched, and fly-fished—good *Anglo* habits that I cultivated early on and which had provided a good balance to the *café con leche, pastelitos and dominos*—genetic traits of *la raza* which Mami and Papi passed onto my brother and me. In my heart it was like I lived with two souls: one great big *Cubaniche* which pulled me towards the mango tree dreams and the sea breezes of Matanzas Bay and the other which was the white-haired, erudite professor-physician I am now. I managed to survive New Jersey, and even succeed, courtesy of the epigenetics of the chameleon, of faith and of the marriage of work ethic with the ever-dangling chip on the shoulder and the grit that got me through it all. Nothing I ever got which was of any significance had come easy to me, which was why I think I learned to be content and appreciative of what I have. What would have happened if my family and I had stayed behind in Cuba? Who and what would I have become? The thought terrifies me and at the same time it stimulates my curiosity.

28
REMEMBERING TO FORGIVE

The day we left Cuba, we were strip-searched before boarding the plane for *Ciudad Méjico*. It was in an opaque glass enclosure with two doors at *Aeropuerto Jose Martí*, one side for the women, another for the men. My abuelo was very frail, he walked with a cane and could no longer wear a belt, so he wore suspenders. I stood behind him in line.

Quítese los pantalones y zapatos, viejo! The young bearded soldier wearing olive fatigues and a pistol strapped to his belt ordered my grandfather to lower his pants and take off his shoes in a gruff, demeaning tone.

Abuelo was a very proper man. He was not used to people being impolite, let alone refer to him as "*viejo*," which I am certain he viewed as disrespectful, especially coming from a younger person who was neither family nor acquaintance. I knew my abuelo well, and although of advanced age, he was fearless, and I could tell by his demeanor he was incensed. I noticed he began to lift his cane slowly and I just knew he was intending to strike the soldier and teach him a lesson. I reached my hand down his flank from behind and gently took hold of his cane.

Here, let me hold your bastón, abuelo, so you can sit and remove your shoes. I looked up at the soldier, *Por favor, official, él és diabético...* I sat abuelo down and began removing his shoes. My father and brother just stood there, motionless. We got through the strip search after I managed to distract abuelo, who by this time in his life had begun to be forgetful and easily confused. The distraction with my grandfather at least took my mind off fretting about the "capsule" I had swallowed earlier.

I will never forget that bearded *miliciano's* face. I often wonder what was the fate of this soldier who so disrespected, manhandled and humiliated an eighty-year-old-man, had him lower his trousers, exposed the old man's privates in front of his grandson, and checked his shoes for contraband. Did this feed his macho? Did he feel like he was protecting the national security of the revolution by frisking a malnourished, confused old man that could have been his own father or grandfather? Was the frisked old man carrying valuable secrets about the revolution tucked in his urine-stained underwear? Did the pistol on the *miliciano's* belt make him feel secure against this clear-and-present-danger geriatric threat to *El Movimiento de la Revolucíon?*

Who knows what may have happened? Maybe the soldier would go on to be promoted with distinction from low-ranked *miliciano* to *sargento* in the *26 of July Movement.* Perhaps he was rewarded by his government with a house unwillingly vacated by some exile *gusano* family who like ours, left the country, tails between their legs. Maybe over the ensuing decade this soldier's family began to have second thoughts about the food they didn't have on their table, or about the propaganda slogans painted on walls and monuments, or about the promises that might never come to pass. Or maybe he was eventually drafted to command a platoon in the jungles of Angola, to be injured fighting against a force that was no threat to his own motherland. Maybe during that conflict, he was wounded and languished on a cot in a makeshift hospital, lying in his cholera-induced watery shit until abdominal cramps and fever pushed him to his last breath, thus bringing an ignominious end to a victory for a power to whom he never swore allegiance. Or perhaps that once *miliciano* became a teacher, raised his family in a quiet town outside of Habana, and in his discontent, became one of the lucky ones years later to board the *flotilla* at Mariel Harbor—a *comunista arrepentido*. Who knows, this enlightened ex-communist might have ended up in Miami or Chicago, or California, enjoying frequent flyer miles, wallowing in his newly-found freedom, and gorging on the fruits of capitalism in America.

* * *

My father would have to take a bus to his new job at the bodega in Union City. The weekend before he started, my cousin Carlos and I accompanied him for a round-trip trial run. As we got on the bus, Carlos paid the fare for the three of us and asked us to sit just behind the driver so we could be sure which stop to get off and be close to the door. Another man got on the bus after us at the same stop, and he obviously knew the bus driver as they struck up a loud conversation. It was a rather spirited to-and-fro between the two. I had no idea what they were saying but it sounded like they were laughing and at the same time ranting about something,

Bus driver (laying on the horn): *These fuckin' Spics... they double park their friggin' cars, blocking the street...they come here and they can't speak the language. Throw garbage on the street, act like they own the damn place, the place is going to shit, I say.*

Passenger buddy (in a thick Joisy accent): *Jeeez what-da-hell do ya expect, dey come in banana boats and all they want is our jobs!*

My cousin Carlos who was at the time fluent and spoke English without an accent became increasingly upset at whatever it was the two were saying. Carlos was a quiet person but I could sense he was about to explode. We barely got off the bus when he started jumping up and down and yelling as the door closed, giving the bus driver the middle finger, and saying things that I would later find out were references to the lubricious interests of the driver's mother, grandmother and wife.

The science of Neuropsychology has elegantly unfolded for us the origin of bias, and how bias can distort thinking, influence what we believe and often sway the decisions we make, the thoughts we have and the judgments we hold. I suspect our Bergenline bus line driver could have been an *Archie Bunker* prototype, and his passenger buddy a perfect foil, both reflecting their upbringings, their experiences and/or ignorance with Cubans-or people of latin descent and culture. Some might say today that these two were right to be allowed to express their opinions freely, loudly, and without consequence in a democratic country such as ours. Others would say they were just two bigots blowing steam.

After Carlos translated the passenger-bus driver rant, I understood his reaction and I became livid. In fact, it was all I could do to keep myself from chasing after the bus and punching the two sons-of-*putas* out. How dare they?

But as papi and mami had taught me, I realized that ignorance is often the punishment of the ignorant. I was sure that the bus driver would have to face my father on that route for as long as they both depended on their symbiotic existence with the bus transit system for their respective livelihoods. I never told my father about the specifics of the incident. I knew papi's innate diplomacy well. Even with a language deficit, I was certain that after *Archie* drove him for forty blocks each way, every day even for a few weeks, by example and with the likeable demeanor my father had, Archie would soften and maybe come to understand that while some of "us" may double-park illegally, and not always speak the language, not all of us throw garbage out the window, and some of us actually arrived at the feet of Lady Liberty, not in banana boats, but in planes, even on ships. Archie might also come to understand that like my father, most of "us" are polite, respectful, law-abiding, and yes, trying to work hard to make life good for our families. After all is said and done, when the science can't explain somebody's *bigotry*, there is always a philosophy that can. I am reminded of a Bahamian aphorism I once heard: *Man is like the monkey, the higher he climbs, the more he shows his ass.*

* * *

In the eighth grade at Elementary School No. 9. I had to suffer through: *Hey, Reechardo, do they speak Cuban in Cuba? Do you have toilet paper there? Are you a relative of Reeeky Reechardo?* I was too embarrassed to go to school dances as I knew I needed to avoid dealing with the anticipated *La la la la la Bamba* and *Can you do the Mexican hat dance*? immigrant jabs.

I would eventually get over all that too. If a person doesn't know that Spanish is the language that is spoken in Spanish-speaking countries, perhaps they should be worried with being understood should the need arise to speak "American" with Britts, Jamaicans or South Africans.

As for issues of *dèrriere etiquette*, we fortunately did have the benefit of toilet paper in most houses in Cuba. Some disadvantaged or extremely poverty-ridden folks sometimes resorted to used newspapers or rags, others in really remote rural areas may have kept strips of banana leaves in their outhouses. I relished telling people who asked me the toilet paper question that I heard rumors that those same banana leaves were sometimes repurposed to pack the bananas that were shipped in banana boats to American supermarkets.

As for Reeky Reechardo, (Desi Arnaz) he and his family fled Cuba in the 1930's because of political persecution. "Reeky" was a superb musician, band leader, actor and television star who revolutionized modern American television. I am pleased to acknowledge that my name and his stage name were the same, and that we shared national origins and height, but that is as far as the comparison went. As for La Bamba, and the Mexican Hat Dance, that could be the subject of two fascinating long essays in anthropology, both of which are beyond my sphere of knowledge.

While in college, couch discussions at the dorms or study halls would occasionally turn to blatant "hispanophobia." I usually ignored getting into the mix of these less-than-intellectual-tangles, but at times my frustration and anger would overwhelm me. After taking a calming breath, I would often speak up in my now near-excellent English accent,

You may not realize that I am Cuban, and I resent your negative comments about Hispanics and Latinos...

That's funny, but you don't really look or sound Cuban... (I would hear that more times than I cared to.) I even developed a canned retort when this would come up,

I'm curious about what you mean. What does a Cuban look or sound like? To which I would generally get no answer...just awkward silence. *Are you Catholic? Protestant?* I would then ask. When they would answer "yes", I would retort, *That's funny, because you don't really look or sound Protestant.*

* * *

During my medical internship at the VA Hospital, one night I was on call. A nurse asked me to come and evaluate a patient with a fever. I spoke to the man. He was a rugged, sun-scorched, North Florida farmer. I examined him, wrote orders for bloodwork, x-rays and medication, and asked the nurse to call me with the results or if there was any further issue. About two hours later I was summoned back to Ward D. The nurse told me that the patient wanted to speak to me, that the man was very upset. After looking at his results, I went back to his bedside to check on him. He had pneumonia. I wrote some orders for antibiotics.

While sitting at the nursing station, the nurse tapped on my shoulder and said apologetically,

I am really sorry about the patient being so upset. I don't know what he said to you, but before you came back I asked him what was wrong and he started screaming: "I want that damned doctor to come back, right now!"

She said she tried to calm him down, *"Do you remember the doctor's name?"*

That damned Mexican doctor, Doctor Godzilla! I had to laugh.

All the unpleasantries and the insults notwithstanding, over the years I learned that in order to rise beyond the pettiness and bigotry of people, it is always best to heal oneself with humor and humility and to embrace a hefty dose of maturity. I always remember to forgive, and so I have finally forgiven. I cannot say I have had the same success with the "forgetting" part, however.

29
OIGAN

The court was called to order. Thirty-eight men and women were seated in the two front rows of the Federal Court room. The judge made introductory remarks. I stood at the podium and with my index finger tapped the microphone twice before I spoke,

"I arrived in the United States as a refugee from Cuba at the age of thirteen and became a naturalized citizen at twenty-two, in the Federal Court in Newark, New Jersey. I neither recall the name of the speaker, nor the substance of what he said. But I remember it as a somewhat long ramble that sounded patriotic.

There is a word in Spanish: *OIGAN*. Spelled O, I, G, A, N. It means "hear this," or "listen." I need for you to remember what I have to say to you today, so I will keep it brief. I will tell you what being an American is for me, highlighting the letters that spell the word *OIGAN*.

The "*O*" is for *Opportunity*. When I came to the United States, my mother and father and my brother and I slept in the same room, in a single house along with relatives. The 16 of us shared a single bathroom. We scrambled to pay bills. I never expected I would be able to attend a university. But Mr. Longano, my high school guidance counselor encouraged me, and helped me make it happen. I received a scholarship. In college, Dr. Von Tienhoven, one of my physiology professors, mentored me and helped me realize I could fulfill my desire to study medicine. A high school English teacher, Mrs. Farley, taught me to write and gave me the love for reading literature. Forty years later, Ms. Leon, editor of a literary magazine accepted my first short story for publication. It had been rejected more than thirty times by other journals. Sometimes you accept opportunity, but most of the time you have to fight for it, especially when you know there are others encouraging you along the way of your struggle.

As I've thought about this, it occurs to me that all of these people who gave me an opportunity were either immigrants or sons or daughters of immigrants themselves. Think about this.

The *"I"* is for *Independence*. I suspect some of you here today have lived in countries where the state controls the press and the television. Where like my father, either you or one of your relatives might have been arrested for simply violating a night curfew. So imagine how liberating it was for me when I came to the United States to see thousands of students marching in protest for civil rights, or for me to write my first letter to the editor of a newspaper stating my displeasure of a political figure without fearing I would be censored or arrested.

The *"G"* is for *Gratitude*. When I first arrived in Union City, New Jersey, I left Cuba with the clothing on my back and one extra change of clothes. The local Catholic Church had a clothes closet in their basement. I received some free clothes, including a sweater which I often wore to school. But I felt awkward wearing it to church, always thinking that the person who donated it might be sitting behind me and would recognize it. I have kept that sweater. It serves as a bittersweet reminder for me of need, of the basic goodness in people, of pride, of humility, but mostly of gratitude. I now wish perhaps the person who donated it would have seen me wearing it after all. You see, gratitude is not just a feeling. It is a symbolic sweater or shawl of sorts, something you always hold close, to comfort you and get you through the difficult times.

The "*A*" is for *American.* This is your day. Today you officially become Americans. With becoming an American comes great responsibility. It will be your charge to learn the language, to teach it to your children and your parents. It will be your task to embrace American culture.

This country was founded on the principles of a participatory democracy. As Americans, in order to preserve the values of our democracy you must participate.

This nation, like many nations has faced cyclical dark periods. For those of you who picked up the newspaper or listened to the news on the way here today, some would say we are in one of those dark periods now. Some would say that the word *immigrant* has become a bad word.

Many Americans born in this country take for granted that it is not just their responsibility, but their duty to participate in democracy. In the fifty-plus years I have lived here, I have seen this nation rise from dark periods but only when people participate, even when it was painful and maybe in doing so, sometimes at great risk. They vote with conviction, they speak up for social justice. I urge you as new citizens of this nation to uphold the principles of our democracy, register to vote and lift our nation on the principles of democracy.

The last letter is "*N.*" It stands for *Never forget* where you come from. As of today, consider that within you are two beating hearts: The heart you were born with, and now your adopted American heart. Your heart, like mine, will learn to beat with American blood. This is part of your transformation. Another way to think of this journey of where you came from is to view your life as a wonderful colorful fiber of cloth. It gives you comfort and warmth. Weave your native fiber it into the tapestry that makes the United States the wonderful and diverse nation it is. I give you my warmest congratulations."

30
GOING HOME

Eight of us crammed into two Russian-made Ladas. *Que direccíon?* asked the driver. *Calle Medio and San Gabriel Street,* I said. He looked at me oddly. *You mean 8 street, corner of 15th...* The streets of many Cuban cities no longer bore the names of historical heroes or saints.

We pulled up to the curb. Reddish pink, not the pastel green I remembered. Bars on the window. The flagstones Papi handpicked for the facade had been painted over with lechada. Number 23 ½, "Old" *Medio* Street. We exited the vehicles, my wife, daughters, and their husbands. A young man stood by the window of what was once our house. Shaved head, bare-chested and in his mid-thirties, he seemed alarmed at the *Americanos* spilling out of cars, with drawn and aimed smart phones and video cameras, lenses panning up and down the street. I approached him in Cuban-slanged Spanish. *Mira, chico...* I explained that I had lived at 23 ½ *Calle Medio* fifty years ago and that my father built this house. A petite, bird-framed woman, probably in her early eighties opened the front door. She stood at the threshold. *Abuela,* said the young man. *Este señor says he used to live here....* Her expression was confusion bordering on trepidation.

Señora...my name is Ricardo. (By now neighbors curiously gathered about and around us.) *I left Matanzas when I was thirteen. My father Pepe owned the grocery on the corner.* It dawned on her that she had been "assigned" the house we surrendered to the authorities half a century ago. It was as if she'd seen a ghost... I continued, *I remember Juanito next door, he used to let me watch him refinish furniture in his shop... And Toto and Billita who lived behind the bakery across the street. Toto gave me pastelitos when I washed his car.*

The woman's demeanor changed. *Juanito died two years ago, as did Toto.* The shirtless young man said, *Abuela, they want to see his old house, permítelos entrar.* I was embarrassed, never intending to intrude. "*No, no Señora, no es necesario.*" She stepped aside, waved us in. A motor scooter adorned the foyer. The grey tiles were the same. So was the pale green paint on the walls except where it flaked. We stepped through to the corner of the living room where our television used to be. The broadcasts from WCMQ were long ago replaced by state-controlled Tele Rebelde. We walked past what was my bedroom. Broomsticks nailed to each corner of the bed tethered a mosquito net. I didn't recognize the furniture. I wondered whether my books and toys might still be behind those closet doors after I begrudgingly closed them fifty-three years earlier. We walked past the bathroom. I recognized the familiar sink where I watched Papi shave. The green porcelain toilet bowl was devoid a toilet seat, and the top of the tank was missing. Absent the soap, shaving brush and razor, the shelf below the mirror over the sink looked the same, but now supported a lone wooden hairbrush with missing bristles. What had been my parents' bedroom was neat but sparsely furnished. A bed and a rocking chair I didn't recognize. My little brother's bed was gone. Where once an image of the Virgin of El Cobre hung, a poster of a generic landscape clung from a single nail above the bed.

My daughter stepped ahead of me into the kitchen. It was as plain and neat as I remembered it. Missing were the short-wave radio and the dining room table. A few dented pots and pans lay prone on a cloth on the counter. I recalled the odor of boiling salted codfish permeating the house, like when Mami used to make it every Wednesday, without fail. Not this Wednesday. I imagined the aroma, but there was no food in sight and the pantry looked bare. I stepped around dirt and tile shards bordering a hole in the terrace where it appeared the plumbing had had some recent emergent surgical intervention. Looking out the roofed terrace into the back yard, the sour-orange tree my grandmother had planted was replaced by a partially dilapidated one-room shack. The flowers she so loved were gone.

On the way out, the side courtyard where Papi used to rock me was bare. The hammock was gone. One rusty eyebolt from which it hung remained. The whole "tour" lasted less than five minutes. My head throbbed with melancholy, anger, remorse, self-pity, then catharsis. It was an odd feeling, like thinking I was about to eat a pickle in the darkness, but it turns out it was an oreo cookie I bit into. I thanked the kind lady. I told her that Mami and Papi would be glad that she had given great love to the house all these years. I hugged her and wished her well, then stepped out to the sidewalk. We turned the corner onto *San Gabriel*. Where Papi's grocery store once stood, was now a barren lot. Our driver said the building had been torn down years ago. I wrapped my face in my hands. As we drove down the street, the sidewalks seemed a lot narrower than I remembered them.

31
EP'ILOGO

When I returned to Matanzas in 2016, I tried to find my abuela and abuelo's house on *San Gabriel* Street. The whitewashed stucco was no longer whitewashed. There were cracks on the façade and deep pockmarks where the stucco had fallen off. The wood on the two-panel front door was bleached gray and splintered and the iron hinges rusted. The lion-head door knockers were gone, and only the rusty scars of the screw holes that once held them remained. A hand-painted sign was nailed on the door with the word *Privado*. The front window had been removed, replaced by planks, and barred. I could not see a roof above the front wall, which made me think the house had collapsed or been torn down. Peeking through a small hole in the door of what was once abuelo and abuela's house, it looked like an empty lot, betrayed by time and overgrown with weeds.

* * *

On a parking lot by the *Monumento de la Revolucíon* in Habana, I saw a navy blue 1951 four-door Chrevrolet, same model and year as mi Tío Yayo's "plum." I thought of him then. Tío died in New Jersey in his late 80's, still smoking four packs of cigarettes and drinking about a gallon of coffee a day. But his epileptic fits were rare in his old age. Looking back with a clinical eye, I suspect Tío Yayo's social clumsiness, adherence to rigid routines, extreme attention to detail, eccentric behavior and aloofness, deep attachments to animals along with his brilliant mind, would nowadays be considered consistent with findings observed in autism spectrum disorder. I will always remember my uncle with great respect. Most of the skills I learned, such as working with tools, drawing, caring for animals, developing good routines, and obsessing over details I owe to him. Yes, he was my mentor and my tormentor. For all of it I am grateful. But I am sorry that it took so long for me to understand and acknowledge that it was he who lived the tormented life.

Matanzas Bay was as expansive and crystal blue-green as I remembered it and the salty breeze coming off the water made me feel at home. The old rusty iron bridge at the mouth of the San Juan river where the sharks used to linger was still there, but the slaughterhouse upstream and the *Plaza Mercado* were gone. I thought of Oscar and Rique's Uncle Samuel's rowboat and our escapade to the bay. There were no Russian tankers this time.

I had heard that Dr. Moorfi and his wife died. A friend of a distant relative had told my mother years ago that both Oscar and Rique might have left the country and that Rique might have died in an accident in Miami. I do not know the whereabouts of my other friends from the *barrio*, nor have I any way to track them down on first names alone.

* * *

I am thankful to Dr. Pancorvo for motivating me to become the kind of doctor he was not. To this day I am aghast how a doctor could have prescribed a narcotic to a child for simple cramps. Perhaps this and subsequent clinical experience in part sparked my interest in medication errors and adverse drug reactions from inappropriate prescribing during my academic medical career. In my practice I scrutinized medications before considering prescribing them, and always made it a habit to withdraw rather than add anything except the most indispensable medications to my patients. The word "doctor" originates from the Latin *docere*, "to teach." Having come from a family of teachers, becoming a teacher of medicine came naturally to me, and as such for thirty-four years I embarked on teaching medical students and residents how to become competent and compassionate physicians. This, along with the appreciation and privilege of caring for my patients, has been a great source of passion and satisfaction in my life. I hope abuela feels vindicated.

After I had my blood drawn and fainted at the laboratory on *San Gabriel and Compostela*, Dr. Pancorvo told my mother I was anemic and he gave me an iron tonic. He also told mami to give me a tablespoon of cod liver oil every day. The iron made me constipated and the cod liver oil was awful to take, especially when it became rancid in the heat. I was constipated and miserable, but I was ready to do anything for anemia, just knowing that I didn't have Uncle Gilberto's leukemia to worry about after all.

I suffered through Dr. Pancorvo during my early years. I am sure that his intentions were good, but I don't believe he was a very kind person by the way he treated people, especially when they were sick. He was gruff and came across as uncaring. In contrast, I so much treasured my abuela's hands-on approach when I became sick, that years later her holistic demeanor prompted me to want to be a doctor. I do have Dr. Pancorvo to thank for making me want to be the kind of doctor he was not.

* * *

Nocturnal eneuresis is what they call bedwetting, or pissing in your sleep when you are a little kid. What I learned in medical school is that this is not a psychiatric disorder, and although some elements of it may be "in your head," it falls within the range of developmental physiologic maturation in kids ages 4-9. More recent data from surveys suggests that children who as toddlers had "difficult temperaments" and problems "adapting" or kids who were "rigid" about routines can be more at risk for bedwetting. Most children get over this issue of bedwetting by age eight or nine.

Bedwetting which doesn't resolve or which persists to a later age or recurs can occur in children who are difficult-to-awake heavy sleepers, or kids with diabetes, attention-deficit and hyperactivity, sleep apnea, tiny bladders or rarer conditions like sickle cell disease or rare neurologic conditions. We are now learning that many kids suffer from circadian (body clock) maturation delay and this causes abnormal secretion of urine-regulating hormones at night and gets better with a hormone treatment. But most importantly, stressing children who bedwet with guilt trips and/or punishment, can only make the behavior worse and really mess with their psyche.

We are living in strange times. In these days of medicalizing just about every human condition as a disease in search of a therapy, nocturnal "eneuretics" have not been spared from their share of being subjected to acupuncture, hypnosis, magnetic sacral root stimulation, massage therapy, chiropractic manipulation- and yes, even tonsillectomy.

I am glad that mami was pragmatic and didn't make a big issue of my urine-soaked payamas. She kept me from drinking fluids before bedtime and gave me lots of love and understanding. She preserved my dignity. The pissing at night eventually went away, she salvaged my self-esteem and saved money by not buying so much detergent.

* * *

It wasn't until several years ago that I learned Ernest Hemingway published *The Old Man and the Sea* in 1952, five years before my brother was born. Thus, it appears that the old man at the clinic on *Milanés* street may have been telling just another great fish tale to an impressionable and naïve seven-year-old. To this day I still wonder where the truth lies, however: the *viejo* was so authentic and believable. It could be argued that one's fiction of one event does not necessarily negate a similar incident which might have taken place in the real-life experience of another, and at a different time.

* * *

Gambling on cockfights is theoretically "illegal" albeit still very alive in Cuba. The Cuban government has sanctioned several official *bayas de peleas de gallos* (cockfighting arenas) throughout the island, including the infamous Diego de Avila Arena in what was the former *Camaguey* Province which seats 1000 people. It is legal to own cocks, to train them to fight, and to fight them. Gambling on the cockfights and the building of clandestine cockfighting pits is banned, but it is said that this is not easily enforceable, so it appears authorities may still look the other way. People still carry their *gallos finos* in slings or burlap sacks under their arms to arenas made of palm fronds. I saw a man transporting a cockerel on his bicycle on the outskirts of Habana three years back and the scene triggered a sickening sensation in me.

* * *

My oldest and very precocious grandson recently turned four and I decided that since we are both getting old, it was time for us to build our first *papalote*. We went to town to buy supplies. On the way back, we stopped at a traffic light on a street which flanks the Annapolis National Cemetery. My grandson spoke from the rear car seat,

But Papi (he calls me Papi), *what are all those white things on the ground?*

That is a cemetery.

I know what a cemetery is, Papi. But what are the white things in a row?

That is a special cemetery where they bury soldiers who die.

But Papi, what's a soldier?

Well...a soldier is a person who wears a uniform and who protects the people in a country from bad people in another country.

But, isn't that the same as a policeman? And why do soldiers die?

Well...because sometimes when soldiers are fighting to protect their country, they get killed by other soldiers during a war.

What's a war?

Well, there was a timely existential question for me. Did I care to explain war to a four-year-old?

Well, you see, sometimes people have wars when they don't like each other. They have a group of soldiers and they wear uniforms and they use flags and then they try to go and hurt the other country's bad soldiers until the other soldiers can't fight anymore. Sometimes during the war, the soldiers from one country destroy the houses of the other people's country and soldiers and people who are not soldiers sometimes die. Sometimes the soldiers take the things that belong to the other people's country and if they can't have them, they break them.

But, Papi, I'm confused...

I saw myself heading quickly down a rabbit hole with a four-year-old! So, I pulled the car ahead when the light changed, and drove into the nearest parking area, put the car in "Park," took a deep breath and just sat there for a brief moment, contemplating answers.

Papi? came the little voice from the rear of the car.

I gazed down at the front seat where I had placed a bag with strips of balsa wood, string, spools, glue, colored tissue papers, supplies needed for building our kite. *Parque René Fragas*. Butterflies. Razor blades. Kite runners. Throwing stones. *Papalote* wars. And now, soldier wars.

I thought about a famous song from the early seventies that speaks to teaching ones' children well, because the hell their fathers went through was miserable, that we should feed them dreams that they can pick from, so they won't know about their fears during tender years, the fears that their elders grew up with...Batista. Castro. Cuban Missile Crisis. Viet Nam. Sandinistas. Damn it, enough!!!

We went home and built two beautiful *papalotls*, a red one in the shape of a diamond, the other a purple and yellow hexagon. It turns out we forgot the typewriter ribbon for the tail. But we are that much closer to that first flight.

* * *

In 1919 during the Bolshevik revolution, Lenin decreed a program based on the philosophy that "Without literacy there can be no politics, there can only be rumors, gossip and prejudice." All people ages 8-50 in the Soviet Union would be expected to learn to read and write, and along with becoming literate, to be infused with communist propaganda.

Forty plus years later, in 1961, Ché Guevara instituted a similar playbook for Cuba. Castro, like Lenin, decreed it. They called it "*La Campaña contra el Analfabetismo*" (The Campaign against illiteracy). Schoolteachers like mami and my uncle were made to make it happen, unpaid for their efforts, but expected to do it for the benefit of the *Revolucíon*, and to promote "*solidarity*" among the proletariat. There was that word I had not known: *Solidarity*! For all these years the *Movimiento* claims it has worked. People were supposedly infused with solidarity and propaganda as they learned to read and write. It is reported that Cuba has the third highest literacy rate in the world. But, contrary to Lenin's philosophy, literacy has neither abolished prejudice, nor rumors, nor gossip. In recent years despite the propaganda some say the solidarity, like the cracking walls of most buildings in Habana, appears to be crumbling. In 2019 the Cuban government launched a program to combat racism on the island. These days, it is common to see very literate young people in the streets of

Habana, hugging the external walls of hotels, hoping to attract *wee-fee* (wi-fi signals on their cell phones) hungry for news from the outside world and eager to wallow in gossip and rumors with their friends.

* * *

Generoso, the seamstress's son was clearly effeminate. He might have been gay. I grew up in a society where machismo and homophobia were permanent fixtures, with residuals even now, not just in Cuba, but throughout most of Latin America. The social norm was to abhor any male who didn't behave like a man. This behavior was learned, drummed into us like propaganda and worse yet, passed on, even by seemingly "decent people." The kids I grew up around, their parents, neighbors, and teachers all share the blame for the intolerance and downright meanness, not to mention the prejudice against people like Gene who, even when trying to express themselves as children, were vilified and disenfranchised, when their only "sin" was that they acted and felt different. The truth is that I, (we) all treated him badly. We excluded him from playing games that "boys" played. We made fun of him. I even tried to physically hurt him. Yes, I got my just dues, my retribution, and I am reminded of it anytime I touch the bony ridge on my nose. I have no idea what might have happened to Generoso, whether he is still alive, or how his life might have turned out. Regardless of his sexual orientation I wish I could apologize in person for my cruelty and ignorance. I would ask him to forgive me. But I wouldn't blame him if he didn't.

Brigade 2506 was the self-appointed name used by the CIA-sponsored paramilitary group of 1400 Cuban exiles, 1202 of whom were captured and 118 who were killed on the Bay of Pigs invasion attempt on April 17, 1961. Those 1400 men landed on the Zapata swamp, only to be surrounded by 20,000 Cuban militia troops. From the outset, the invasion force never had a chance. Some U.S. military attaches who helped train the Brigade 2506 soldiers felt that president Kennedy betrayed the exiles by pulling back U.S. firepower to back the mission at the last minute.

In the small rural town where I now live in North Florida, I met a fellow Cuban exile. Now in his late seventies, he was 18 when he joined up as one of the youngest soldiers in the 2506 Brigade Bay of Pigs invasion. He was captured after being wounded, was imprisoned by Castro's men, and eventually released to the United States. I suspect he might have been hogtied and paraded as a *traidor de la revolucíon* in one of the trucks that went up my street in Matanzas after capture. We might unknowingly have crossed paths fifty years ago, me as a child bystander and he, atop a truck, bloodied, sunburned and mosquito-bitten beside his fellow prisoners.

After mami passed away in 2015, while sorting through a trinket box of her belongings, I found a brown plastic toy soldier with a missing arm. I cannot be sure if it was the cake soldier, I thought I left behind at the Habana airport on the day we left the island.

* * *

At age 92, mami had two of her poems published in a well-respected literary journal at around the same time when I struggled to get my first story accepted by a publisher, any publisher. Her persistence and encouragement was a great lesson for me, and her love for words as well as my respect for her creative genius is what motivated me to write this chronicle. She gave me the impetus to write in the nonscientific arena and to explore fiction and creative nonfiction as well as poetry. Writing about my childhood has been a way for me to look back and backfill with great memories some of those empty spaces that the void of her leaving this world created for me.

* * *

The *Hotel Marlowe* on *Independencia* avenue in Mexico City is still standing. Transformed into a three-star chic boutique hotel, its "unpretentious and un-air-conditioned rooms" now cost $204 a night for five adults and two children in one room. The last recorded earthquake in Mexico City, lasting 20 seconds was in September of 2017. *Angelita's Cantina* up the alley off *Dolores street* no longer exists. The parking lot where Victor and his family lived is now a tourist mall and modern multilevel parking garage.

* * *

When I attended Elementary School No.9 in the 1960's there were probably less than 20 Hispanic/Latino students out of a thousand in the school. Back then, E.S.O.L. (English as a Second Other Language) programs were non-existent. Had there been ESOL, it might just as well have stood for "Expect to Survive Or Lose." Now of about 1000 students, 88% are Hispanic/Latino. I suspect that while Fire Drills are still actively rehearsed, there are probably no nuclear bomb exercises held at School No.9. I would also surmise that nowadays most students don't know what a divisor or a dividend is, and probably don't care, as they all have calculators.

The IQ tests administered in schools are still used, but cautionary caveats about "guessing" answers, "having a bad day," anxiety, motivation, rapport with the examiners abound, as does knowledge that economically disadvantaged students, or from ethnic minorities, especially if English is their second language, generally receive lower scores. The experts blame this on the tests, not the students. The major rhetorical question is, should administrators and teachers administer IQ tests in English to children who do not speak the language? *Locos.* I hope they have adjusted.

The bully that attacked me while in elementary school, went onto the same high school I attended in New Jersey. We never interacted since the day by the synagogue on 85th and 4th and fortunately for me, we were not in the same classes through all four years. I actively avoided him at school events, in the hallways and in the locker room. On the day of our high school graduation, someone tapped me on the shoulder from behind. As I turned, there was Tommy in his cap and gown, facing me. I had a horrible flashback and could barely hold back my anxiety. He looked at me directly, then extended his hand and wished me luck.

When I went back to Matanzas recently, I tried in vain to find a way to get to what might have been Juanito's parents' farm. After half a century, no one seemed to know nor could they give me directions without my having more specifics, especially since the farm was out in a rural area with few officially named roads.

After Fidel Castro took over Cuba, the Reforma Agraria came, and many small farmers surrendered their property to government cooperatives so people did not always stay on the family farm. I did not know Juanito's last name and since both my parents had both passed away and had lost contact with his family since leaving Cuba, I was unable to get details that would help me track them down.

Time and circumstances have betrayed me. So I am left to chronicle these memories, the mango dreams, and the hopeful thoughts that maybe Juanito and I might one day cross paths again. Recollections, like dreams are often a conglomerate of what may have actually taken place, and by nature are only as accurate as the mind is willing or able to retrieve for us. It was no coincidence that Jorge Luis Borges brought Funes to my attention, for it prompted me to jot my childhood memories before it might have been too late. I feel blessed with these great recollections and with having at least in part, the opportunity to bring some of them full-circle. My childhood could not have been better. I'm glad I was able to trace my steps and I can't help but wonder how it might have been, had destiny and circumstances not exiled me when they did.

It isn't often that dreams rescue us from the stark reality of missed opportunities and regrets. I like to believe the mango tree still stands by the stream. Perhaps one day I will find it.

ACKNOWLEDGMENTS

"Bienvenido" Hispanic Culture Review, Vol XXVI 2019-2020 p60-63. (May, 2020)

"Lagrimitas" Lunch Ticket Magazine www.lunchticket.org Antioch University's Literary Magazine (December, 2017)

"Peeling back the burlap," The Bellingham Review, Vol 41, issue 76, (Spring 2018)

"The Hot Water Bottle." Humanism Evolving Through Arts and Literature (HEAL Magazine), 5, 16-17.

"Cuca la Muda." The Acentos Review, Summer, 2013. Retrieved from https://www.acentosreview.com/August_2013/Gonzalez-Rothi.html

"The Seventh Angel." Acentos Review, Winter 2012 Retrieved from https://www.acentosreview.com/February_2021/Gonzalez-Rothi.html

"Papi and me" www.bioStories.com featured essay May 2017

"Going Home" www.foliateoak.com May 2017

Running Wild Press publishes stories that cross genres with great stories and writing. RIZE publishes great genre stories written by people of color and by authors who identify with other marginalized groups. Our team consists of:

Lisa Diane Kastner, Founder and Executive Editor
Cody Sisco, Acquisitions Editor, RIZE
Benjamin White, Acquisition Editor, Running Wild
Peter A. Wright, Acquisition Editor, Running Wild
Resa Alboher, Editor
Angela Andrews, Editor
Sandra Bush, Editor
Ashley Crantas, Editor
Rebecca Dimyan, Editor
Abigail Efird, Editor
Aimee Hardy, Editor
Henry L. Herz, Editor
Cecilia Kennedy, Editor
Barbara Lockwood, Editor
Scott Schultz, Editor

Evangeline Estropia, Product Manager
Kimberly Ligutan, Product Manager
Lara Macaione, Marketing Director
Joelle Mitchell, Licensing and Strategy Lead
Pulp Art Studios, Cover Design
Standout Books, Interior Design
Polgarus Studios, Interior Design

Learn more about us and our stories at www.runningwild-press.com.

Loved this story and want more? Follow us at www.runningwildpress.com, www.facebook.com/runningwild press, on Twitter @lisadkastner @RunWildBooks